Metaflux

Photocopy of photograph of 'Gays Against Imperialism' at the
Belgium Embassy Dublin in protest of the teaching ban against
Eliane Morissens, circa February 1982, Photographer Unknown.

Courtesy Irish Queer Archive, National Library of Ireland

Metal button in support of the Eliane Morissens Solidarity Committee, distributed during a demonstration in Ixelles, Belgium, 27.03.82.

Courtesy Amsab Institute of Social History, Ghent, Belgium

A Quare Invisibility 9

Scenes with Cathal Kerrigan:

    INT. PHONE CALL – AFTERNOON 53–80

    INT. LIBRARY – MORNING 81–88

    INT. GAY BAR – NIGHT 89–96

    INT. APARTMENT – NIGHT 97–104

    INT. HOTEL – DAYTIME 105–116

    EXT. RAISED GARDEN – MORNING 117–130

    INT. TERRACED HOUSE – EVENING 131–136

    EXT. BUSY STREET – DAYTIME 137–154

Chart of main LGBTQ organizations referred to
with (proximity) linkages by Cathal Kerrigan 155

Detail Index 157–164

Colophon 166

A Quare Invisibility

The Irish intonation of the word queer is quare; as in 'unusual, baffling.' My great-grandmothers, Bridget Ford or Mary Murphy, might have taken to calling a particularly odd person a 'quare hawk'. The most popular use of the word occurs in Brendan Behan's 1954 play, *The Quare Fellow*, where the title character remains invisible throughout the performance and is solely rendered by what other characters say about him. Set in Mount Joy Prison, the play takes place on the days bookending the execution of *Quare Fellow*, whose framing in the speech of others reveals the hypocritical morals underlying modern forms of judgment and (in)justice. There is a quare distinction made between murder by a silver-topped cane or a butcher knife, with the knife being more deplorable than the cane *only* in light of the class aspirations the evidence represents. Written in an English muffled by echoes of imperial erasure, the exchange at the introduction of Behan's camp character, the *Other Fellow*, ballasts the invisibility of *Quare Fellow* by baring everyday intolerance at the edge of laws and words:

OTHER FELLOW. My God! Is this what I've come to, mixing with murderers! I'd rather not, thank you, though I could do with a smoke. I'll have to spend long months here, even if I get my remission, with murderers and thieves and God knows what! You're not all murderers are you? You haven't killed anyone, have you?

PRISONER B. Not for a while I haven't.

OTHER FELLOW. I cannot imagine any worse crime than taking a life, can you?

PRISONER B. It'd depend whose life.

OTHER FELLOW. Of course. I mean, a murderer would be justified in taking his own life, wouldn't he? "We send him forth" says Carlisle — you've heard of Carlisle haven't you? — "We send him forth, back to the void, back to the darkness, far out beyond the stars, let him go from us."

DUNLAVIN. [HEAD OUT OF DOOR OF CELL] Oh. I thought it was Healy from the Department or someone giving it out of them.

PRISONER A. Looks like this man is a bit of an intellectual.

DUNLAVIN. Is that what they call it now?[1]

It is the *Other Fellow's* animation and inflection that leaves his character open for a dual incarceration—both in socially punitive architecture *and* in the act of pre-judging a private sensibility through naming it. That is, naming one that warrants 'othering' before and after the fact of listening. In asking, 'is that what they call it now,?' the insult against the other is made possible. That is, the insult of *having* to be called anything at all. In the violence of this *first impression* — of being named before being heard out — the intellectual appears in the script as a proxy to what they are not calling *it*, with any future actors having to interpret what, exactly, *it* is.

What is now known as 'Queer' evolved from what they used to call it. The reclamation of insult is the ground upon which its theory stands. A curtain-call reclamation of language from the double incarceration of speech, the Queer entered the dignity of mainstream, prominent discourse, dissolving clear (national) borders and even the notion of a singular, stable subject.

By the late 2000s, the discourse around the Queer had become bogged down in the coded institutionalization of speech acts — because there is

---

1. Brendan Behan, *The Quare Fellow*, London: Bradford and Dickens, 1961, 14–15

certainly imperialism at play in first impressions. The Queer's liberatory potential was dampened, even popularly despised, first and foremost as a threat to a banality firmly established in everyday speech. Wouldn't any current liberatory project then have to find words to unite the worker, the queer, and the doubly incarcerated all at once? Freeing them all from conservative constraints such as those that might frame 'them' as being a manner of lifestyle at best, or choice, at worst? Impoverished complaints such as these might normally be expressed in tandem with exasperation — perhaps with the accumulating spectrum — at having to *learn* and *use* a vocabulary that expands both before and after the fact of listening.[2]

It is not surprising then that the intellectual is disdained, just as the queer is, because *both* cause frustration to those who simply refuse to continue thinking.

> SEDGWICK. 'Remember the fifties?' Lily Tomlin used to ask. 'No one was gay in the fifties; they were just shy.' Queer, I'd suggest, might usefully be thought of as referring in the first place to this group or an overlapping group of infants and children, those whose sense of identity is for some reason tuned to the note of shame. I mean that in the sense I can't tell you what it is — it certainly isn't a single thing [...] And can anyone suppose that we'll ever figure what happened around political correctness if we don't

---

2. See Günther Anders: 'Our technological environment, the world of our devices, which consists of monsters, is either featureless, nondescript and inconspicuous, or it is deliberately kept out of sight. Anyone who has imagination to rely on instead of eyes, which nowadays no longer are of use, sees that it is precisely this invisibility, the invisibility of the monsters, which is the monstrosity of today. This invisibility transforms us into beings whose lives blindly pass by the machines, because we still have a most obsolete trust in our eyes. This at least, until the day when we will no longer have any time to realise that today our eyes cannot be trusted.' Quoted from Christopher John Müller's *Introduction to Günther Anders's 'The Obsolescence of Privacy'*, Counter Text 3.1, Edinburgh University Press 2017.

see it as, among other things, a highly politicized chain reaction of shame dynamics?³

I wore nail varnish in my back garden once in 1990. Simply liked the way my nails looked, casually turning the wheels of an upturned bike emulating the dashboard, steering wheel and gears of a car. I can't remember the colour of my nails; the bike was red and yellow, I think. I know I loved the glisten of my hands turning the pedals, the position of which was equivalent to the gears in a Renault 4. So that's what I had, a Renault 4. I remember looking forward to seeing how the nail varnish might look handling messages. ('Can you drive downtown for the messages' is my favourite Irish slang for 'running errands.') There were parts of me that shouldn't be seen in public, and so, as in any (kind of) play, humiliation was a violence easily avoided. The nail colour was erased. Faced with the weight of histories, their applications and removals, these tiny digits seem meaningless; yet they point to something very specific about the *threat* of even the smallest aesthetic gestures in public life.

Looking back on it, one of my first impressions of the violence of public naming was also the beginning of my understanding of solidarity. I remember feeling real confusion when the kids in school called *quare* kids, mostly me, a Lydia. Not calling me 'Lydia,' but 'a' Lydia. Beginning in 1997, Lydia Foy endured gruelling notoriety, fighting a 20-year legal battle with the help of Free Legal Aid to have her birth certificate changed to match her gender. I grew up in the same town, then, as a legal icon; and sometimes it was 'we' called in her proper name. Micro-vernaculars carried Lydia's name on the weight of words, spoken from the violent comfort of making equivalence between obvious others. This naming, this calling, cries out against nothing other than the danger of the *other* as the interruption upon which falls the desire for pink *or* blue — not *and,* never *both* — and certainly never bleeding to purple. We can't all be queer like Prince.

Once I exchanged hellos with Lydia in Jacob's corner shop. My heart pounded like Australia to Abba. In 1997, she grew the tallest foxglove flower in the world, and I had wanted to make a bronze sculpture

---

3. Eve Kosofky Sedgwick, *Touching Feeling: Affect, Pedagogy, Performativity,* Durham/London: Duke University Press, 2003, p 63-64

commemorating it. But, as Agnetha Faltskog said of Australian obsession: 'it's a thin line between celebration and menace'. In the end, I felt that making the foxglove emblematic would be like trespassing in a garden I am unwarranted to be in, let alone assume the right to represent. So, perhaps the transience of 1997s tallest foxglove is best represented by a sculpture that started and stopped for so long; it never amounted to more than fragments of material tests. Faced with the lightness of history, it is possible 1997s tallest foxglove is *unarchivable*, save for its insufficient but evocative scientific category: *Digitalis Purpurea* (Lady Glove).[4]

In 2014, I began looking at material in the Irish Queer Archive. Earlier that year, drag performer Rory O'Neill, alias Panti Bliss, appeared on the Saturday Night Show. O'Neill used the word 'homophobia', or 'homophobic', to describe the activities of the Catholic Conservative Iona Institute, who were actively lobbying against marriage equality. The anti-marriage lobby premised their argument on the prejudicial belief that marriage was a privilege *only* intended for the heterosexual reproductive unit (the baptism machine of the Roman Catholic Church). In its secular state, love is much more complex, and marriage essentially becomes a dual identification in 'tax brackets'. Yet, following O'Neill's appearance, National Broadcasting Agency RTÉ paid €85,000 in damages to the Christian Iona Institute, as well as journalists John Waters and Breda O'Brien (Iona's Patron). The trinity of injured public figures had in fact actively campaigned for marriage rights to be reserved exclusively for heterosexual reproduction; *and*, they successfully sued RTÉ under Ireland's defamation of character laws. The truly crucial points around marriage as a legal construct were drowned out by perpetrator-victimhood, and the argument that marriage should never come to represent a threshold to proper citizenship was left entirely unexamined in the debate.

On the stage of the Abbey Theatre in Dublin, Panti Bliss responded publicly to RTÉ's legal vindication of implicit and concealed homophobia, exposing and condemning the fact that those who have felt oppression are

---

4. IQA MS 46,007/1, 16.02.98 Lydia Annice Foy from Athy Co. Kildare, sends a handmade card to Ailbhe Smyth, Director Women's Education and Research Centre (WERC), University College Dublin, thanking her for a great conference. Photocopy pages of poems written by Lydia are also included with the card.

disallowed the right to call it thus. Oppression, as Panti argued, is not just supported by culturally ingrained homophobia in Irish society. It is also internalized in homosexuals themselves — that is, in their *shame*. The RTÉ libel suit *merely* created capital from words already broadcast and heard. Its 'after the fact' sanitizing of words did not contribute to civic argument; it *merely* threatened the removal of a word from a vocabulary where conflict needed to occur: at the level of everyday speech. Oppression is not a question of what, but when, regardless of what or who it is called.

> PANTI. As you may have gathered, I am painfully middle class. My father was a country vet, I went to a nice school, afterwards I went to that most middle class of institutions, an art college, and although this may surprise some of you I have always found gainful employment in my chosen field: gender discombobulation. So the kind of grinding, abject poverty we saw so powerfully on stage tonight, is something that I can thankfully say, I have no experience of. But, I do know a little something about oppression. Oppression is something that I can relate to. Now I am not of course for a minute going to compare my situation to Dublin workers in 1913, but, I do know what it feels like to be 'put in your place'.[5]

Ireland's Defamation of Character Law was the means by which the word 'homophobia' was revoked from a broadcast speech; almost pathetically, certainly desperately, John Waters, Breda O'Brien and the Iona Institute used the most secular law for capital, not moral, gain. Their karma was definitely a Drag Queen. In the Irish Queer Archive, the more I found out the less I felt I knew. The history seemed too close. Other researchers were handling hundreds-of-years old material, dried out and brittle, and here was I, handling paper comparatively moist, almost steaming. A photocopy at the periphery of the archive stopped me. It was filed under the 'General Papers' of 'Charles Kerrigan', whom I would later email and

---

5. *Panti's Noble call at the Abbey Theatre — WITH SUBTITLES*. Published 02.02.14. http://www.youtube.com/watch?v=WXayhUzWnlO (last opened 05.12.18).

The Irish Times (1921-Current File); Aug 31, 1981;
ProQuest Historical Newspapers: The Irish Times
pg. 9

PINK TRIANGLE

Sir,—The recent correspondence on the placing of a symbolic pink triangle on a mountain in Munster by the Irish Gay Rights Movement leads me to commend those who are willing to put their energies into the struggle for gay rights. However, I would suggest that those energies would be better channelled in working for a united gay movement to fight attacks on gays. For some years now I have been involved in the gay liberation movement; a constant barrier to progress for the past four years has been the division within the gay movement with two rival groups (the National Gay Federation and the Irish Gay Rights Movement) wasting precious resources by duplicating services and competing for support.

The recent judgment in the Norris constitutional case and the letter from Mr Fowler (August 6th) denying Nazi persecution of gays are two examples of the growing opposition we gays will have to overcome in order to win our rights. We can only fight effectively if we are united. Therefore, I call on IGRM and NGF to publicly commit themselves to a united gay movement. — Yours, etc.,

CHARLES KERRIGAN,
Phibsboro,
Dublin.

phone call. Up to that point, however, my impressions in the archive play out as a series of acts.

I

I felt a quare invisibility in the Irish Queer Archive pointing toward everything not marked by its narrative retention. Like any archive, but especially a queer one, it is haunted by all that it doesn't say about the history and future it names. There is, after all, always going to be the pre-queer history of private sensibilities, as inaccessible and *unarchivable* now as they were then. The history of the West had never been one of progress, but rather the progress of erasure; so it occurred to me that the 'Queer' couldn't have a timeline other than a ghostly one, anyway, as archives merely mark the success of time's progression.[6]

Perhaps moves to digitalize and educate around the Irish Queer Archive might not be given priority over more popular commemorative campaigns such as 'The Centenary' or the 1916 Rebellion — that sensationalist moment between terrorism and liberation in the birth of this historically conflicted Republic. Perhaps, if history has proven anything definitively to me, it is that phenomena are rarely birthed by fashion or by name, and that there are always hidden histories, even of history. So, far from being a novel one, the Irish Queer Archive appeared as one of many micro-histories tracking the nuance of identity politics and their social enterprise in Europe. What surprised me about the politics in the Irish Queer Archive was in retrospect not remarkable at all, especially given how the last years have unfolded. What we overidentify with presently as 'neoliberalism'[7] plays out at the very beginning of the 1980s.

---

6. The Irish Queer Archive was officially integrated into the National Library of Ireland in 2008, at the cusp of an economic crash.
7. See definition of Chantal Mouffe in *For a Left Populism*, London: Verso 2018, p 12: 'Neoliberalism is the term currently used to refer to this hegemonic formation which, far from being limited to the economic domain, also connotes a whole conception of society and of the individual grounded on a philosophy of possessive individualism.'

UNITED GAY MOVEMENT

Sir, — Charles Kerrigan's appeal for a united gay movement (Letters, August 31st) is certainly thought-provoking. In looking at this question, though, do we mean a unity on paper between existing groups or real unity of heart and clarity of purpose among their organisers? We believe that our main task should be the achievement of the latter and we have repeatedly demonstrated our genuine commitment to this ideal in various ways.

National Gay Federation delegates in large numbers participated in a conference at Glencree on the theme of reconciliation within the gay community; the first National Gay Conference earlier this year again saw heavy attendance and participation by NGF when much discussion centred around the question of unity. The tremendous feeling of solidarity evident among all present has led to real goodwill and growing co-operation between at least two groups attending, NGF and Munster IGRM. NGF has also taken initiatives to open dialogue with the re-formed Irish Gay Rights Movement, but the ensuing discussions were terminated unilaterally by the latter group; we very much regretted their decision to withdraw and remain well disposed towards further dialogue with any interested representatives.

These two major groups, the National Gay Federation and the Irish Gay Rights Movement (re-formed in 1979), do indeed, as Mr Kerrigan points out, provide a range of services to the gay community. Duplication of amenities meaning that a choice of social venues now exists should perhaps be seen as a good thing; it is questionable, however, whether the setting up of an additional telephone counselling service for gay people to compete with the long-established independent Tel-A-Friend (01-710608) can be viewed in the same light. (Surely those offering such help do not have their own ambitions uppermost in mind?) Duplication of political work in the gay liberation field, besides wasting resources of time and energy, very likely does lead to confusion in the public's mind.

The aims of the two major organisations as outlined in their constitutions are almost identical (in practice, the re-formed IGRM has chosen to place greater emphasis on "social" as against "political" work), and it cannot be denied that with few exceptions the people involved at organisational level in both have sacrificed much to bring about improvements in the lives of gay people. Surely it should be possible to acknowledge that both organisations share common roots in the original Irish Gay Rights Movement (1974-78) and to use this as the basis for a genuine co-operation?

Any impetus towards the united gay movement Mr Kerrigan desires would be greatly aided by the collective opinion of ordinary gay people and the moral force this can bring to bear making itself felt, so that, although the process may be painful to those who have an emotional investment in maintaining the present "separate development", the aspirations of Irish gays for a united national gay movement may be brought nearer realisation.

Mr Kerrigan's call for a public commitment has been noted; the National Gay Federation's response to this challenge has always been consistent: NGF believes in the ideal of a truly united gay movement and commits itself to continue to do all in its power to unite the hearts and minds of all gay people so that together our united efforts towards gay liberation may be made ever more effectively. — Yours, etc.,

BERNARD KEOGH,
General Secretary,
National Gay Federation.
Hirschfeld Centre,
10 Fownes Street Upper,
Dublin 2.

A SQUARE MONTH

Sir,—I suppose your readers were so busy looking for palindromes that they missed the significance of Sunday, September 27th. This was the second occasion this century, and the last one, when the day multiplied by the square root of the month is equal to the year which in turn is the month squared. Surely a day to have lived through!—Yours etc.,

MAURICE DEVANE
44 Charleston Road,
Dublin 6.

PINK TRIANGLE

Sir, — I refer to Mr Kerrigan's call for "effectiveness" under the heading "Pink Triangle," (Letters, August 31st).

The Irish Gay Rights Movement's campaign for real homosexual equality has, over the years, been characterised by the politicisation of ideals to be implemented by cohesive effort leading to an identifiable effect on the social and legal standing of homosexual life-styles in this country.

In this context, one of our prime objectives, as embodied in our constitution, is the realisation of positive public awareness "by education and example." This is a full-time and ongoing process, but Mr Kerrigan seems instead to suggest that we in IGRM have both the time and inclination to indulge in time-wasting posturing. Not so; he should understand that we are a voluntary organisation drawn from working people who relfect the Irish gay potential. Naturally, we welcome concrete support in fulfilling. our countrywide campaigns and in providing the established social and information centres (maintained regularly since 1974). We already have unanimity of purpose; Mr Kerrigan suggests some sort of uniformity under duress and this is not in keeping with his socialist traditions, and could dilute our effectiveness. — Yours, etc.,

SEAN J. CONNOLLY,
National Chariman,
Irish Gay Rights
Movement,
18 North Lotts,
(off Bachelors Walk),
Dublin 1.

II

By the late 1990s and early 2000s the *male* coming-out narrative was more opportunely articulated by the intellectual success of Queer Theory in the enclaves of Western academia. Gay liberation is, after all, a success story of the *free market decades*, giving birth to 'child-unburdened' economic trends such as the 'pink pound' or the 'Dorothy dollar.' Terms such as these only lightly concealed the class and racial ignorance of the 'so 90s' equation that sexuality = market. In 1998, the BBC's Business Correspondent Richard Quest reported

> QUEST. When it comes to doing business, few tradesmen care about the colour of your money, so long as it is real.
>
> *Continuing*
>
> QUEST. One class of cash has a very distinct name. In Britain it is often called the Pink Pound, in the US the Dorothy Dollar [...] Many figures quoted have to be taken with a pinch of salt — after all it serves the gay press to promote the community. Even Marketing Week acknowledges, "the problem is that no-one knows how big the market it is." [But] as the recent House of Lords vote that rejected the lowered age of consent shows, PR hype is often well ahead of public acceptance.[8]

The cynical logic of identity capitalism overplayed by Quest underlies the *first-impression*[9] logic that underscores cognitive advancements in capitalism

---

8. Paul Quest, *Business: The Economy and The Pink Pound*, reporting in London for BBC Friday 31.07.98. http://news.bbc.co.uk/2/hi/business/142998.stm (last accessed 09.10.18)
9. The 'first impression' logic of cognitive capitalism is based on the manipulation of consumer and social activity by algorithms that replace knowledge with information. This operates on many political levels,

generally. As communication and community became corporate, digital terms, the 21st Century equation whereby identity = capital quickly set fatigue in motion. Precisely as a result of market-led assumptions that merely dressed discrimination as profit. There is a terrifying impression that this market-led tolerance and thinking only ever found 'liberation' in a *merely* liberated patriarchy. That's perhaps why 'Liberation' has become an increasingly slippery term, given that one freedom, or singular right, has never guaranteed the freedom of another, or room for the rights of the many. Twenty years after Quest's pre-2000 optimism, humanity is faced with the truly terrifying impression that identity is the only infinite resource on this Earth, which is rapidly depleting, toward no time or thinking at all.

> BOTTICI. The paradox of a world full of images but deprived of imagination; this rests on the growth of the more passive side of the imaginal, which happens at the expense of its more active side. Otherwise said, we are so image saturated by the spectacle clamour for screen time that it becomes increasingly difficult to create new ones. [...] Many authors have noticed that elections have always had the function of a ritual, since, by virtue of mere repetition, they enforce a certain model of society by providing it visible continuity. But today the quantity of images that accompanies elections in most Western countries has become such that the spectacle prevails over the content.[10]

---

manipulating the 'first impressions' of 'screen time' wherein identity comes to mean 'malleable prejudice'. One of many cogs in this machine is news headlines written solely to inspire 'rage sharing', not close reading.

10. Chiara Bottici, *Imaginal Politics: Images beyond the imagination and the imaginary*, New York: Columbia University Press, 2014, p 111-112. In this book, Bottici identifies the 'imaginal' as an intermediate domain between the privacy of the imagination and the public of the collective imaginary.

III

Queer Theory emerged at the very end of the 1980s from the direct actions an intersectional community took against the homicidal State Policies of the AIDS epidemic. The heteronormative market trends that followed in parallel brought with them a very particular form of privatisation. So identity itself became a competitive stake, leaving no room for a public mourning, just the positive affirmations of *following*.

It is not surprising then that the 'Queer' comes with economic and spectral baggage, having had no place or time to unpack. Yet Queer Theory still clears thinking space for addressing Marxism's early inability to account for the role of desire in the worker's life. That is, the private, emotional excess of the individual that the market so successfully consumes reconfigures and saps. Yet even the blindsiding, masculine excess of the Left was not the biggest shortfall of Marxist abstraction. The biggest? Its failure to account for the invisibility of domestic and reproductive labour as the base of an originary oppression. This is the scene of enforced femininity enclosed by the marital 'I do'. Reinforced by the future silence of friends who would have had to object, there and then, or forever hold their peace. This burden of great-grandmothers — that mainstay of sexuality in the possession of family names— is historically threatened by the limp wrists of men who might seem to trespass, symbolically at least, but only to the point of messing up that Freudian dream of 'playing house.' The question of what a Queer economy might look like, when asked, needs to be asked seriously, especially with regard to how *care* might reconfigure production[11]. Left popularly unanswered, the open wound is salted by the all-too-seasoned idea that the market produced desire alone.

> FEDERICI. The separation of production from reproduction created a class of proletarian women who were as

---

11. Care that is not only care for the other, but care for the Earth itself as the only possibility of co-existence with the other. See also, *Global Justice and Desire: Queering Economy* (Eds. Nikita Dhawan, Antke Engel, Christoph H.E. Holzhey, Volker Woltersdorff) London: Routledge, 2015

dispossessed as men but, unlike their male relatives, in a society that was becoming increasingly monetized, had almost no access to wages, thus being forced into a condition of chronic poverty, economic dependence, and invisibility as workers. The devaluation and feminization of reproductive labor was a disaster also for male workers, for the devaluation of reproductive labor inevitably devalued its product: labor-power.[12]

IV

My quare route though the Irish Queer Archive tracked a conflict that emerged between activism and the social economy of a scene that existed at the edge, and in spite of, the law; a place the *Other Fellow* haunted. To begin at the centre of the Irish Queer Archive is to start with the 1975—1993 legal campaign for the de-criminalization of sexual acts between consenting males. It was led by people who are still speaking, albeit differently, today; cue 1981 President of the *National Gay Federation*, David Norris.

> NORRIS.   It would be an appalling irony if the net impact of the gay liberation movement was merely to make homosexuality safe for capitalism.[13]

Contemporary Queer Theorists might seem to agree with Norris, for the most part. The irony is clear and hardly in need of overstating. Albeit tempting to read Norris's irony as a revolutionary premonition in 1981, his comment was probably rooted in a much more local event, named the *Glitter Ball Wars* by civil rights campaigner and city planner Kieran Rose.

> KERRIGAN.   It was called that because of an argument over which of two opposing factions in the Irish Gay Rights Movement would take possession of a disco ball. For Kieran — and others — it symbolised the

---

12. Silvia Federici, *Caliban and the Witch*, New York: Autonmedia, 2004, p 75
13. IQA MS 45,936/9

farcical tragedy of a split with no real basis other
than personality differences. I have always found
it difficult with progressive left politics because so
much is reactive and defensive. I was in the middle
of the Irish Gay Rights Movement split, and spoke
at the meeting where it all happened. I had friends
on both sides and argued that political activism did
not exclude social pleasure, and in fact it was part of
it. These false dialectics, Political vs Social, Defence
vs Vision, Against Vs For, gives the high ground
to our opponents: Pro-life and the imperialism
behind the Peace and Stability rhetoric of neoliberal politics etc. This is another reason why the
Gays Against Imperialism banner in the photocopy
seems eloquent, and was consciously so. Máirtín
and I wanted to present a vision of what we wanted
to attain — some would say a Utopia.[14]

What ever it meant, the *Glitter Ball War* was symbolic of a larger disagreement that resulted in the fracturing of the movement into splinter organizations, such as the *National Gay Federation* (whose early logo incorporates the organisation formerly known as the *Irish Gay Rights Movement 1973—1978*). The *National Gay Federation* went on to operate a social club, the *Hirschfeld Centre* in Temple Bar, running discos and other social events. Yet the same internal conflicts —perhaps of interest— lingered from the *Glitter Ball Wars* as by January 15th 1982, the *National Gay Federation's* Youth Liaison Officer Kevin Caroll had this to say:

> CARROLL.   I am sure there are many of you who would not necessarily agree with what I say, but I find that we seem to be confusing what constitutes a social achievement and a political issue. I would regard the purchase of the Centre as being a social achievement, but have we recently achieved any political objectives? I see several possible roads the new organisation could take, the most extreme and distasteful having

---

14. Cathal Kerrigan, printed feedback to Gaze Against Imperialism November 2017 Draft.

occurred already in one of our fellow council minds, that being the collapse of National Gay Federation as a political body, and Hirschfeld Enterprises continuing to run the Disco for its own sake. The second is a split between the Political and social elements of the National Gay Federation, and the third is a great re-awakening of a spirit which was present at the time of the David Norris Law case. [...] Let's stop "Playing Politics" internally and turn our attention to the world outside.[15]

Less than a week later in the outside world, on the 20th of January 1982, Charles Self, a set designer at RTÉ, was brutally murdered at his home. The lack of 'forced entry' evidence gave the Police the *first impression* that Self had invited his killer in. The impact this had was that Self's domestic space was reduced to a site of his sexuality *in general*, and not the site of his murder in specific.[16] The *technical* illegality of Self's visibility as a gay man prompted the assumption that his murder must have occurred within his 'scene.' This led to law enforcement questioning 1500 men; all identified as 'suspects' on the basis that they had sex with other men. 1500 suspects, that is, because their sexual history was the only 'evidence' for a theory of cause and effect, of naming and of death.

> ROSE. Many of the questions had nothing to do with the murder, but with the private lives of those being questioned. They were asked who they slept with,

---

15. IQA MS 45,936/2
16. See artist Nairy Baghramian in conversation with Jörg Heiser, Frieze, 2010: 'I'm interested in the political implications of interior design; namely, why certain designers – mainly women and gay men – withdrew so markedly from the public realm of architecture or urban planning to concentrate on the domestic sphere [...] Historically, access to the public sphere has been denied to women and gay men in numerous ways, whether they were not allowed to vote or had to hide their sexual orientation. So it's important to discuss the politics of interior design.' https://frieze.com/article/room-live (Last accessed 9.10.18)

Charles Self Murder Investigation

The Administrative Council of NGF has from the beginning adopted a policy of full cooperation with the Garda Authorities investigating the circumstances of Mr. Self's recent tragic death, while at the same time respecting the confidentiality of names and addresses on our Membership Register.

(The Membership Register has not been made available to the Gardai and access to it has not been requested despite some newspaper reports).

We have in addition asked NGF members to cooperate fully on an individual basis and particularly to come forward voluntarily with any information they might possess that may be of assistance to the Garda inquiry.

Any such information can be passed on through the Garda Confidential Telephone number Dublin (01) 804495.

A number of disquieting reports have reached the NGF National Office to the effect that a small number of individual Garda detectives are employing investigative methods which are not in line with normal Garda procedures.

While we urge members of the gay community to assist the investigation, if possible, we feel that the individual's rights in dealing with the Gardai should be made clear.

Remember!

* You must, if requested, give your name and address to a garda.
* You are not obliged to answer any other questions.
* You are not obliged to accompany the gardai, or to go yourself, to a Garda Station unless you are being arrested.
* If you decide to go voluntarily to a Garda Station it is best to make an appointment a couple of days ahead and be accompanied by a friend when you go. If you wish, a NGF Council member will accompany you.
* When you arrive at the Garda Station ask the Station Sergeant to note your presence and time of arrival in the Station log book.
* Ask and note the names of the garda officers questioning you.
* You are not obliged to answer any questions or sign statements.
* As a rule it is best not to volunteer any information concerning your sexual behaviour as it may incriminate you — REMEMBER IF YOUR SEX LIFE IS GAY, IT'S ILLEGAL.
* You are not obliged to give your fingerprints.
* You are not obliged to allow your photograph to be taken.
* If you go to a Garda Station voluntarily you may LEAVE AT ANY TIME.
* If you are being arrested you must be informed of the reason for your arrest. IMMEDIATELY contact a solicitor
* or the NGF Legal Subcommittee by phoning DUBLIN (01) 710939. Do not answer any questions (except your name and address), give fingerprints or allow your photograph to be taken until your solicitor arrives.
* Do not necessarily accept Gardai advice regarding the choice of a solicitor.

Guidelines for Dealing with the Gardai

When dealing with the Gardai you should be polite but firm regarding your rights.

If you go voluntarily to a Garda Station you should decide which questions you wish to answer or whether you wish to give fingerprints or have your photograph taken.

If you feel it is not in your own interest or in the interest of your friends to answer any particular question, to have your fingerprints or photograph taken be firm but politely refuse to comply with the request.

If you feel you are being harassed or threatened by any individual Garda Officer you should object, have your objections noted by the Station Sergeant and leave the station.

You may make a formal complaint to the Garda Authorities with NGF's support if you wish.

Being in a Garda Station can be frightening, being accompanied by a friend, knowing your rights, and being polite at all times will help you to cope with this situation.

Issued by the National Gay Federation.
February 1982.

> names and addresses of gay friends and even what they did in bed. [...] Many people were threatened that if they did not go voluntarily to the police station, the Guards would turn up at their homes or at their workplaces, with devastating results for those who were not out.[17]

What amounted to a profiling campaign against gay men founded urgent protest against the irony of one law being used, not just technically, as the *evidence* for breaking the most sacred of ethical imperatives: to sustain the life of the other. No official proceedings appear to have been brought against these generalized suspects, possibly due to the fact that activists saturated the media with knowledge of the Police dossiers. It is hard to gauge just how much this affected the lack of prosecutions though, as Self's murder remains unsolved to this day. 'Get your filthy laws off my body' and 'Blame the murderers, not the victims', are two banners on photocopied photographs in the Irish Queer Archive. 'Destroy our dossiers demand gays in Self murder probe', headlines an article in the Sunday World. Looking back from the 21st Century I can see how proximate this case is to the international injustices performed by men in suits[18], that is, to all those places where law enforcements continue to contaminate scenes with nothing but evidence of their own discriminations.

DUBLIN LESBIAN AND GAY COLLECTIVE.

> Our analysis of the situation focused on several areas for immediate reaction. The first of these was the inadequate information being distributed to the gay community. A leaflet issued by National Gay Federation left out one of the most important points: that people could refuse to go to the police station and were not obliged to give any information. Following discussions with National Gay Federation, a new leaflet was drafted outlining

---

17. Kieran Rose, *Diverse Communities: The Evolution of Gay Politics in Ireland*, Cork, Ireland: University College Cork Press, 1994, p 19
18. In an email exchange with Polly Gannon writing from St. Petersburg, she wrote 'when men put on suits, other people become invisible'.

excesses of the Gardaí and basic civil rights for those held in police custody.[19]

V

On March 20th 1983, The Sunday World reported an anti-violence protest that occurred the day before. Its headline read, 'Marchers protest over gay bashings.' The anti-violence protest was spurred by a gross miscarriage of justice reported as a reaction against three youths who received suspended sentences for the murder of Declan Flynn. Airport worker Flynn was beaten to death in Fairview Park, a well-known cruising area in Dublin city centre. Kieran Rose writes that the legally exonerated gang sang 'We Are The Champions' by Queen on a victory march to the Park.[20] To the scene of the crime, *walking free*!

The Flynn family protested at Declan's name being associated with the protest at all, counterclaiming he was not a homosexual, but had been mistaken for one.

> SUNDAY WORLD. A spokesperson for the National Gay Collective[21] [sic] explained yesterday that he died because people thought he was gay. In deference to the family's wishes, The National Gay Collective, organisers of the march, removed Mr. Flynn's name from the leaflets publicising the march.

---

19. Dublin Lesbian and Gay Collective, *Out for Ourselves*, Dublin: Women's Community Press, 1984, p 193
20. Kieran Rose, *Diverse Communities: The Evolution of Gay Politics in Ireland*, University College Cork Press, 1994, p 2
21. 20.03.83. Sunday World article further confounded the layers of implied 'misunderstandings', as the organisers of the march are misnamed in the article as 'National Gay Collective'. The *Dublin Gay and Lesbian Collective* actually organised the march, yet this amalgamation of its name with the *National Gay Federation*, while factually confusing, is illuminatingly so given that all the gay organisations shared similar goals, albeit using different political approaches.

Marchers protest over gay bashings

Scene of the march yesterday. Picture— Myles Byrne.

GAYS and "non-gays" joined forces yesterday [in] a march through Dublin in protest over violence against homosexuals and women.

The parade, of several hundred strong, proceeded from Liberty Hall to Fairview Park where last year a young man was brutally beaten to death by a "queerbashing" gang.

Yesterday's demonstration was organised after gay and other groups reacted angrily when the youths responsible walked free from a Dublin court after getting suspended sentences for manslaughter.

But the family of the victim, 31-year-old airport worker, Declan Flynn, protested at his name being associated with the march, pointing out that he was never a homo-sexual.

A spokesman for the National Gay Federation explained yesterday that Mr. Flynn's sexuality was not the issue. But the fact that he died because he was thought to be gay was the issue.

In deference to the family wishes, the National Gay Collective, organisers of the march, removed Mr. Flynn's name from leaflets publicising the march.

One of the people closely associated with the demonstration told SUNDAY WORLD:

"Essentially we are protesting over violence against people, especially gays and women, and people who are mistaken for gays.

"One of the people attacked by a queerbashing gang in Fairview was an Irish Press journalist, and he was not gay."

He said they had received support for the demonstration from a range of groups, including student groups, the Anti-Amendment Campaign, the Workers Party and Jim Kemmy's Democratic Socialist Party.

Fashion Show

TWINK returns to her old school, St Louis High School, Rathmines tomorrow night at 8 o'clock, to compere a Fashion Show in aid of the school building fund.

It takes place in the School Hall, Charleville Road.

Jail term for whispering 'daft'

THE Irish-born father of a soccer fan jailed on Friday for whispering in court said yesterday that the decision was "daft".

As Manchester United fan Michael O'Farrell, 29, was starting his seven day jail term his father Ray said: "They could have fined my son on the spot. That would have been the right sentence and it would have shut him up.

"But to jail him was harsh, especially because it was so trivial an offence. It was harsh of the magistrate and it was daft."

Mr. O'Farrell of Hazel Grove, Hatfield, Herts, said: "My son is Manchester United mad.

"I just hope he can get out in time for next Saturday's Milk Cup final because he has got a ticket for the match."

It was at Clerkenwell court in London that Michael O'Farrell an unemployed bricklayer, upset magistrate Mr. Mark Romer.

After ignoring a warning not to talk in the public gallery he was arrested by police.

Later, wearing his Manchester United colours, he appeared in the dock and was jailed for contempt of court.

Mr. O'Farrell, 59, said: "It may have been that he was celebrating St. Patrick's Day on Thursday and was still a bit boisterous when he appeared in court."

Demonstration

A demonstration to highlight the plight of Soviet Jews will be held this afternoon outside the USSR Embassy in Dublin.

Sunday World 20/3/83.

This was no mere misnaming or public insult. Declan Flynn succumbed to the name they called him. His public 'outing' was insufficiently averted by the Flynn's family shame, because death is the ultimate border of political life, when the speaking body can no longer represent itself as other.

DUBLIN LESBIAN AND GAY COLLECTIVE.

> Essentially we are protesting over violence against people, especially gays and women, and people who are mistaken for gays.[22]

Refraining from mentioning Declan by family name, the leaflet advertising the march read

> Since the judgment, much has been said about the leniency of the sentences and many have called for the judge's resignation. Little, however, has been said about the hypocrisy that underlies the decision. The only reason for Justice Gannon's leniency is, that despite his denials, he did accept the excuse that the gang were in the park to clear it of homosexuals. This gang has admitted more than twenty cases of planned assault and robbery, choosing as its victims' gays or people they thought might be gay. This premeditation should make the crime more serious, not less.
>
> [...] Because all gay male activity is illegal, the thugs in this case felt justified in beating and eventually killing people they thought of as "queers". Their activities were known to the police; detailed complaints had been made but nothing was done. [...] It took a young man's death to spur them to action.
>
> Suspended sentences would be a welcome and overdue reform in our legal system where pointless and damaging prison sentences are so often given. However, when almost the only step in this

---

22. Sunday World newspaper, 20.03.83

direction is taken in a murder case where the criminals only excuse is "queer bashing", then that is a travesty of reform. [...] There are other cases where prejudices are equally shocking. Some years ago a judge allowed as a "mitigating" factor the excuse that the murdered victim was only a prostitute: in many rape cases an excuse is accepted that the women contributed to the crime by not protesting enough or by being in a dark street by herself. There must be legal reform: these miserable prejudices must not form part of it.

WE DEMAND: The immediate repeal of all legislation that defines us as criminals.

The support of all political groups with concern for human rights.

The participation in this important march of gays and lesbians alike.[23]

VI

Back in 1982, in the wake of the Self murder investigations, the differences of opinion that fuelled the *Glitter Ball Wars*, and whatever future it symbolized, continued to seep in from the outside world. Discontent in the *National Gay Federation* around the 'net impact' of the gay liberation movement was again the subject of a September 1982 speech by David Norris (now named Political Co-ordinator).

NORRIS. The first thing anybody occupying the position of a Political Co-ordinator notices is that the duality implicit in the organisation as a whole is also reflected in its political aspect. [...] The problems encountered here reflect the same spectrum ranging from idealism to bitchiness, integrity to idiocy,

---

23. IQA MS 46,051/1

reflected in human society at large, i.e.: groups such as tennis clubs, pigeon fanciers, railway enthusiasts, etc. However, I should sound a warning note. Whereas if a club of the nature specified collapses through internal wrangling or the ineptitude of officials there are easily available alternatives. It is not my experience that a comparable range of options exists as yet for gay people. Fortunately we are not at the moment plagued with such difficulties, although the schismatic tendency of the Irish temperament should always be borne in mind. In this context I look forward eagerly to the Report of the Commission of Enquiry into the relationship between the National Gay Federation and Hirschfeld Enterprises. [...] However, the example of Raoul Wallenberg should alert us to the fact that nothing excites suspicion in the human animal as effectively as genuine altruism.[24]

For what was, in reality, a small community organisation, the *National Gay Federation* and *Hirschfeld Enterprise's* administrative deposits in the Irish Queer Archive reflect an almost governmental, state mentality. The archive contributions make visible the functioning of a bureaucratic centre surrounded by a fragmentary but influential paralegal periphery. There seemed to have been no alternative to the fact that the activities of the *Hirschfeld Centre* funded the political activities of the legal reform campaign; the two organizations, seemingly at odds, remained two arms of the same body. The schismatic temperaments that Norris mentions inevitably spring and spill unrecognizably into the status quo, in the light of which is the aforementioned variety of interests for the heterosexual (with the nuclear family at its base).

It is also not surprising the activities of the social and political elements of the *National Gay Federation* are so detailed and complete, given that in his 1981 'Presidential' speech, Norris forwards a motion to establish an archive to create the coming gay history. These recollections of schismatic facts in this history of gay liberation might suggest that the success of gay

---

24. IQA, MS 45,936/10

male identity, while admittedly the organizing centre of the Irish Queer Archive, is not in fact a stable 'given'. It is as much about performing in part of a particular economy as it is about legal self-determination. There is always the question of the closet — the 'non scene' of the 'scene' — so 'enterprise' would always read as troublesome as the foundation of liberation here. It *would* be an appalling irony if the net impact of the gay liberation movement would merely to have made homosexuality safe for capitalism.

VII

At the edge of familial confinement, devoid of archival economy, the 'lesbian' was the 'she' never legally named. Lesbianism was never illegal as — when the Victorian laws were drawn up — it was thought that no such carnal act existed. Was it merely Queen Victoria's inability to conceive, in Sappho's delicate terms, of two females with 'shining ankles clad in fairest fashion'?[25] Or was it a deeply engrained sign that the erasure of female sexual sovereignty marked one of the most hypocritical constructions of our time?

On September 7th 1983, a few months after the Fairview March in Dublin, a public referendum giving the unborn foetus equal rights with that of the mother passed successfully in Ireland. Although abortion had been illegal in Ireland for more than a century before, the Amendment functioned to revoke any legal and ethical interpretations of the law, essentially constituting the female reproductive organ as a subject of State authority. The 66.9% majority referendum in favour of the 1983 8th Amendment to the Constitution was arguably a sign of Ireland's ethno-national, Catholic Republic, the second-wave Roman imperialism that effectively recolonized the Republic through the erasure of female

---

25. Ref. to fragment from the *Poems of Sappho*, which is very likely an invocation to Aphrodite, from the Scholiast on Aristophanes' "Peace," 1174; Pollux about A.D. 180.
    A broidered strap of beautiful Lydian work covered her feet
    Her shining ankles clad in fairest fashion
    In broidered leather from the realm of Lydia
    So came the Goddess

GAA – GAYS AGAINST THE AMENDMENT

G.A.A. – GAYS AGAINST THE AMENDMENT

We are asking you to vote "NO" in the forthcoming referendum. Almost all the gay organisations* in Ireland have affiliated to the National Anti-Amendment Campaign, and the G.A.A. (with members from all these groups) is working to ensure that this commitment is translated into <u>votes</u>.

Constitutions deal in Absolutes. No exceptions are allowed, either by the Dail or by the Courts. If the proposed Amendment is passed then:-

: no help whatever could be given to rape victims to prevent an intolerable burden after an already dreadful crime.
: the very limited civil rights to contraception will be drastically reduced. The I.U.D., and many essential types of contraceptive pill will be banned outright.
: the capacity for any citizen to interfere with the private lives of others (via a legal injunction) will be increased appallingly.

It is a standard joke, and a stupid one, that all this is a problem of no concern to gays. But it is:- all of us know married gays, there are many gay fathers and lesbian mothers, and lesbians are no more immune to rape than any other women in Ireland. Less, possibly, given the agression with which they have to deal. Gays are affected, and gays should vote "NO".

The Amendment is opposed by people from all sides of Irish society. By Trade Unionists, and by the Irish Congress of Trade Unions itself; by the Irish Council of Civil Liberties; by Protestant Churches; and by all people concerned with basic civil rights. Some of these people regard the present stringent laws against abortion as necessary; some do not; but all are united in seeing the Amendment as utterly unnecessary as an attempt to introduce into our law an <u>unchangeable</u> element of narrow sectarian legislation.

In the words of one of the opposing groups:- "We believe that the Amendment could be the basis, through litigation or other legal action, for a degree of State interference with personal and sexual privacy and medical ethics unparalled in any country in the Western world", (a statement, remarkably, by the Methodist Church Council).

It seems to us inconceivable that gays could be anything but horrified at such a prospect. It should also be unnecessary to point out that proponents of the Amendment are also those who most vehemently oppose gay rights. Everyone in G.A.A. is against the Amendment. Many of us also support, or belong to, the Womans' Right To Choose Campaign, which proposes simply that it is the right of the individual woman, and of nobody else, to have control over her own body and of her own fertility. We see this as an identical stance to our own declaration as gay people that we alone have rights over our own bodies, and what we shall do with them: we deny the right of anybody else to tell us what we may not do.

Whether or not you agree with this Right To Choose, the importance of voting "NO" is overwhelming. The other questions involved are the concerns of the normal processes of democracy. They must not be pre-empted by a dogmatic insertion in the Constitution.

*N.G.F., L.I.L., Dublin Gay Collective, Irish Lesbian Conference, National Gay Conference

GAYS AGAINST THE AMENDMENT P.O. BOX 1076 DUBLIN 1

The Anti-Amendment Campaign needs money, and it needs it now. Make a contribution by coming to:- G.A.A. Party, Anti-Amendment fund-raiser, Hirschfeld Centre, 10 Fownes St., Dublin – TUESDAY 22nd FEBRUARY, 10 – 3 a.m. £2.00 (£1.50 unwaged) FOOD, WINE, VIDEOS ETC.

sexuality. In 1983, the oppressive history of Roman Catholic Institutions in Ireland might not have been popularly acknowledged, but it would certainly have been a backdrop for hushed conversations, not to mention for understanding the organised imperial hypocrisy that was the baptism machine.

> MCCLINTOCK. The male ritual of baptism — with its bowls of holy water, its washing, its male midwives — is a surrogate birthing ritual, during which men collectively compensate themselves for their invisible role in the birth of the child and diminish women's agency. In Christianity, at least, baptism reenacts childbirth as a male ritual. During baptism, moreover, the child is named — after the father, not the mother. The mother's labors and creative powers (hidden in her "confinement" and denied social recognition) are diminished [...] In the eyes of Christianity, women are incomplete birthers: the child must be born again and named, by men.[26]

The 2018 public referendum removing the 8th Amendment to Irelands Constitution was voted for by a public referendum with a 66.4% majority, perhaps reflecting the religious, not generational divide. Back in 1983 when the 8th Amendment entered the constitution, the *National Gay Federation's* public non-alignment with the Anti-Amendment campaign signalled much broader divisions along class and gendered lines. In 1983, scriptwriter Joni Crone[27] sent a hand written and drawn pamphlet to the *National Gay Federation*, suggesting a more horizontal approach to its

---

26. Anne McClintock, *Imperial Leather: Race, Gender and Sexuality in the Colonial Contest*, London: Routledge, 1995, p 29. In this part of her book, McClintock is comparing the surrogate birthing ritual of baptism with the imperial act of discovery.
27. See for example, Joni Crone, *Anna Livia Lesbia*, theatre play, Splódar Theatre Company, 2017. 'Largely autobiographical, the play centres on the appearance of the author, Joni Crone on *The Late Late Show* in 1980 when she became the first lesbian in Ireland to 'come out' publicly on television.' www.hawkswell.com/events/event/anna-livia-lesbia (last accessed 20.12.18)

'management'.²⁸ The title of Crone's pamphlet is *'Gay Days and Nights of the Roundtable: How to slay the minute-dragon and matters arising (or the structure of the NGF Administrative Council*²⁹*)*. Twelve years later, in 1995, Crone published the following:

> CRONE. A series of educational workshops were held, to illustrate how the 1861 Offenses Against the Person Act had been used against gay men and all women in preventing them from making adult choices about their sexual lives. A vote was held within the National Gay Federation and a majority voted in favour of affiliation. This would have shown public solidarity among gay men and lesbians on the right to choose issue. But a minority of influential and vocal men cited a sub clause in the original document detailing the aims and objectives of National Gay Federation which gave the steering committee the right to over turn decisions of the members in exceptional circumstances, 'in the best interests of the organization'. This betrayal of lesbian and heterosexual women who had campaigned previously for gay male law reform resulted in lesbians leaving the National Gay Federation. And it was the last time that many of us chose to work in any official

---

28. IQA MS 45, 936/11. Knowing that the National Gay Federation's leadership overturned members decisions to align with the 1983 8th Amendment Campaign, I was confused reading a letter written by Eamon Somers on 26.03.83 during his three year phase as *National Gay Federation*'s President. Somers' writes: 'One particular aim I had was to remove the apparent mystique of the Administrative Council, to break the "them and us" syndrome that was a feature of the early *National Gay Federation*. I think, indeed I know, that from Councils point of view some of that is gone and what remains is going quickly. If it comes back it will be because the members actually prefer an aloof Council - a Council which is not bothering gay peoples complacency with the petty realities of running a campaigning and social group.
29. IQA MS 45,936/12

3

NGF Council

PRESENT STRUCTURE

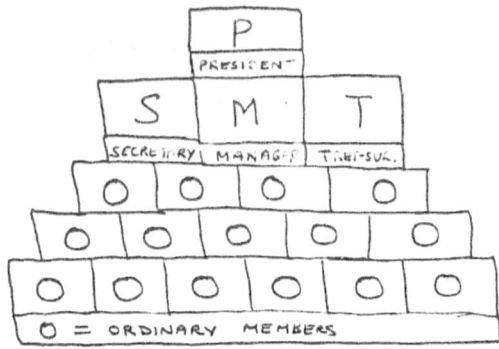

O = ORDINARY MEMBERS

MAINTAIN
FOR
BUSINESS
MATTERS

HIERARCHY
= PYRAMID
OF POWER

RIGID

EFFICIENT

CONSERVATIVE

LIMITED

FUTURE STRUCTURE FOR WORKSHOPS ?

90 MINUTES

2 FACILITATORS

10 MINS.: INTRO
          TOPIC

BREAK INTO
2 GROUPS OF 9 each

50 mins: DISCUSSION

30 MINS: CONFER
         EXCHANGE IDEAS
         PLAN FUTURE
         ACTION

CIRCLE

= EQUAL
  PARTICIPATION

FLEXIBLE

SUITABLE FOR G*
POLITICAL C.R.

ALTERNATIVE PAT*

NO LIMITATION ON *

capacity in solidarity with gay men.³⁰

After 1983, there seems to have been a bitterness running throughout the activist scene, which became too fractured, paralegal and excessive to ever be contained in manuscripts. In this sense, there is something queer in general about Ireland's current, reparative State — if political correctness is, as Sedgwick has it — a highly politicized chain reaction of shame dynamics.³¹

Internationally, the case for women's rights has moved much more slowly than those of gay men in places like Ireland, whose ethical and social infrastructure was deeply rooted in a popular liberation from the oppressive function of the Roman Catholic Church. This is not exclusively a problem of Catholicism, but perhaps of imperialism more generally. The historical snail's pace of women's rights similarly mires due congratulations for 'gay rights' in countries such as India.

> HUMPHREYS. In Turkey and North Africa, in Pakistan and the Muslim world as a whole, neither same-sex anal inserters nor those who engage in fellatio appear to be stigmatized. [...] Men tend to be condemned as "cocksuckers" only in societies that have been strongly influenced by the sex-negativism of Judaeo-Christian tradition. [...] If homosexuals are stigmatized primarily because they are thought to betray the basic, masculine role of being the penetrator, then it is clear that a major factor in the fear and condemnation of male homosexuality is the more generalised abhorrence of women.³²

---

30. *Lesbian and Gay Visions of Ireland: Toward the Twenty-first Century* (ed. Îde O'Carroll and Eoin Collins), London: Cassel, 1995, p 68
31. Eve Kosofky Sedgwick, *Touching Feeling: Affect, Pedagogy, Performativity*, Durham/London: Duke University Press, 2003, p 64
32. Laud Humphreys, *Misogyny As The Source of Homophobia*, from spoken paper presented at the Pacific Sociological Association 05.07.79. *Humphreys Papers Box 13.3*, ONE Archives, Los Angeles.

VIII

As James Penney writes in his highly polemical critique of Queer Theory, 'some people simply cannot afford to come out.' This is Penney's unsubtle allusion to how the 'Coming Out' narrative itself has been co-opted by a not-so-inclusive doctrine of economic success, pointing out, as others do, Queer Theory's inability to account for non-sexualised forms of marginalisation or exclusion as they map the fiscal terrain.

The assumption that the 'Queer' had become a matter of 'mere' lifestyle was then flawed from the start, as here was an unquestioned standard for leveraging difference. But was it only ever leveraged on the reduction of the 'queer' to sexual communities whose visibility is in turn leveraged by their socio-economic success? By the second decade of the 21st Century, and usually by combining Marxism with Psychoanalysis, theorists such as Penney place Queer Theory under scrutiny, not only for its focus on the ever adaptable individual, but also for the success of 'gay liberation' in the niche social enterprises of conservative politics.

Beyond the violence of these naming games, there is the much colder, harder case of justice in the domestic sphere — where theory is lifted from life. In 2009, Penney writes a particularly detailed critique of phenomenological trends in contemporary Queer Theory. He picks up, or rather sits down at, Sara Ahmed's 'table' argument with conservative gay theorist Bruce Bawer.

> AHMED. Bruce Bawer argues in *A Place at the Table* (1994) that gays and lesbians should desire to join the big table rather than have "a little table all of our own" [...] Bawer also describes a queer desire for "little tables" as the "ethos of multiculturalism," where "each accredited victimhood group" is given their own table. It is interesting to note here that the "big table" evokes the family table (where we come from), and also "society" itself as a "single table". Bawer's rejection of queer "subcultures" hence calls for a return to the family table [...] To join this table enacts the desire for assimilation: in the sense of becoming

a "part" of the family but also becoming like the family, which is itself predicated on likeness. What is in this desire to be placed at the table?

We could agree with Bawer that a queer politics is not about laying new tables, whatever their size. After all, to set up new tables would leave the "big table" in its place.[33]

PENNEY. Left unexplored in Ahmed's rejoinder is the invigorating and authentically subversive possibility that when the queer subject insists on sitting at the family table, the nature of the table itself, the logic by which it operates, changes. The at-the-table-queer forces others to re-examine their understanding of family. Even more importantly, queer self-inclusion exposes the family's own difference from itself — that is, the ways in which its members have already transgressed the patriarchal rules according to which the family is officially supposed to function. [...] Bawer's gay conservative contingent is left to dominate discussions as they are left unchallenged as the token gays at the grownups' table.[34]

This issue of alliance and overspeaking has been a reoccurring motif in the world's civil rights movements, especially as it pertains to gendered difference. Edited by Dublin Lesbian and Gay Collective in 1986, the book *Out For Ourselves: The Lives of Irish Lesbians and Gay Men* pointed out these very invisibilities and blind spots in the representational politics of Ireland's gay legal campaign. The book claims that while the legal situation was indeed used as a 'backdrop of oppression', its predominance often ignored the vital connection gay rights had to identities falling outside male exclusivity.

---

33. Sara Ahmed, *Queer Phenomenology: Orientations, Objects, Others*, Durham, USA: 2006, p 173-174
34. James Penney, *After Queer Theory: The Limits of Sexual Politics*, London: Pluto Press, 2014, p 23

DUBLIN LESBIAN AND GAY COLLECTIVE.
> None of this legislation applies to lesbians. Not because lesbianism is more acceptable, but because at the time the laws were drawn up women were thought not to have sexuality at all, let alone one that operated independently of men. This point clearly indicates that lesbians take their position in a society from the general position of women. As a result they suffer whatever discriminations women suffer as well as those discriminations that arrive specifically from being a lesbian. Nor does the exclusion of lesbian sexuality from the legislation mean that they suffer any less oppression. Lesbians suffer as much, if not more, discrimination as gay men as a result of their sexuality. Clearly, then, law reform itself will not solve our problems.[35]

The under-discussed split between gay rights and feminist movements internationally, even within the left, was in fact being addressed as far back as the late 1970s. Radical, pre-queer theorist Mario Mieli combined psychoanalytic with Marxist analysis to attempt a conceptual liberation from the patriarchal hold of Eros (of heterosexuality as the gauge of success). Mieli sought to move on from repeating the heterosexual norms that would become popularly known as homonormativity, which *was* liberation, but only to a point. This struggle is not just fought on the biological body, as there is also the corporeal violence pertaining to the gendered assignment generally.

MIELI. Eros also finds liberation via the creation of new erotic relationships between women and gay men. This is in no way a question of reforming the Norm. Heterosexuality is essentially reactionary, because, being based on the contradiction between the sexes, it perpetuates the phallocentric male, the prototype of the fascist male that the state, and the Left within the system, always propagate.

---

35. Dublin Lesbian and Gay Collectives, *Out for Ourselves*, Women's Community Press, Dublin: 1984, p 191

> Revolutionary homosexuals reject heterosexuality as a norm, as the base of the family, and the guarantee of male privilege and the oppression of women; they combat it, recognizing it as a form of sexuality in the name of which the system has attacked homosexuals and incited people to persecute them.[36]

The steering committee of the *National Gay Federation* overruled a majority vote to publically support the 1983 Anti 8th Amendment campaign. Why would this support be at odds with a minority who had self-given 'foundational' power to overturn the 'will' of a majority? What is in 'the best interests' of gay liberation then? What net impact does it have? In his 1982 speech Norris offers clarifications.

> NORRIS. We all wish for a united and healthy gay movement. This, however admirable in itself is merely a prelude to the really important work of gay liberation in the wider context. Let me say here I am absolutely committed to the continuation of National Gay Federation as a one-issue organisation. I say this with the wisdom of hindsight. National Gay Federation and its predecessors developed from a broadly based sexual liberation grouping precisely because none of these movements ever adequately reflected the needs of gay people. Nor indeed could they. Nevertheless from time to time an influx of new temporarily energetic and idealistic new blood may seek to redirect our energies into these diffuse issues. It is of course healthy and proper that we should debate, but I hope you will bear with me while I make my own position clear. This is that I will oppose any move to sacrifice political achievement on the altar of self-indulgent ideological purity. [...] I do not wish it to be thought that I am suggesting a selfish individual indifference on these

---

36. Mario Mieli, *Homosexuality and Liberation: Elements of a Gay Critique*, translated by David Fernbach London: Gay Men's Press, 1980, p. 186–187

issues. In fact as many of you know I was myself a
signatory to Anne Colony's Contraception Bill,
have long been outspoken and active against Capital
Punishment and am one of the sponsors of the
Anti-Amendment Campaign.[37]

Keeping Norris's due integrity intact, it is nevertheless clear that he is indeed satisfied by the recognition of people hearing *his* public voice. Yet *his* political personality alone did not represent, or satisfy, the many voices that make up any growing community. That women's sexual sovereignty over their own bodies was considered incompatible with *legal* reform for male homosexuals is, sadly, not surprising given the patriarchal inheritance of the times. There is, however, a deep irony if the success story of gay liberation came to rely on the mechanisms of a lightly veiled patriarchy. Perhaps *gay* history itself must then be considered and approached as a form of masculinity in the name of which all the other naming games continue. So does the recent history of gay liberation, or more so its historicisation, then also present us with the problem of a *merely* liberated patriarchy?

IX

In the 4th Century BCE, there was an ancient army called *The Sacred Band of Thebes*, unique in its mythology, in that it was composed of one hundred and fifty couples of male lovers. The alignment of male coupling with tactical power was based on the logic that the lovers would not forsake each other in battle. Stronger in mono pairs, this band of lovers would still have had to match the ideal soldier's body. *The Sacred Band* is not a myth of tolerance or virtue. Here is a myth of political expediency for the continuation of imperial power. As a dramatic optic of a certain political structure, the imperial sacredness of an army of gay lovers exceeds imaginations of mere tolerance; lurking behind which are often undisclosed intolerances that at various points of history repeat as volcanic displays of violence along class and gendered lines.

---

37. IQA MS 45,936/9

The merely liberated patriarchy of *The Sacred Band* was destined to be one day unsuccessful as *it* had come to mean 'progress'; but only up to a point.

In the 21st Century AD, Jaspir K Puar resists the dominant, mono-issue right. Puar focuses her resistance on male gay commentaries that followed CBS's publishing of photographs proving the rape and torture of prisoners at the hands of American soldiers in Abu Ghraib. CBS News had published the photographs in April 2004 and forever destabilised the free and liberal façade of America's 'home front'. Puar deconstructs the imperialist roots of these mono-issue reactionaries, isolating their 'overspoken-ness' from the sacristy of their merely liberated patriarchy.

> PUAR. To foreground homophobia over the other vectors of shame — this foregrounding functioning as a key symptom of homonormativity — is to miss that these photos are not merely representative of the homophobia of the military; they are also racist, misogynist, and imperialist.[38]

Like the Pink Pound, myths such as *The Sacred Band* all maintain the unjust historical realities inherent in the gender binary[39]. Bound as it was to the 'either-or' of pink or blue, passive or active, loved or beloved, product or consumer. The 'don't ask, don't tell' policy is similarly embittered with its own liberal — as long as nobody talks about it — success. This success is aligned with perpetual states of war waged against the *other* who is always somewhere else, while — in the meantime — sons and daughters return home carrying fewer limbs but the same family names.

My quare impression of the Sacred Band — not unlike the engraving on Thomas Hobbes' Leviathan — is concerned, under a certain gaze, with how loving bodies are used politically, regardless of the private experience of sex. Hobbes' infamous image articulated the dual dependence of political obedience and the maintenance of peace, where the survival of the

---

38. Jaspir K. Puar, *Terrorist Assemblages*, Duke University Press, 2007, p 94-95
39. See Julieta Paredes, *Hilando Fino Desde el Feminismo Comunitario (Spinning Fine Thread: Perspectives from Communitarian Feminism)*, Mexico: Cooperativa El Rebozo, Creative Commons, 2014

Emperor is equivalent to the survival of the petrified body politic. Hobbes often described himself as being born the twin of fear, as his mother had given birth to him prematurely. Her labor was induced by the news of upcoming war. So it was the devastation of civil war — a threshold to which being matricide — that fuelled Hobbes anxious philosophy of contract and alliance.

There is a photocopy of a photograph near the edge of the callable section of the Irish Queer Archive, filed under the 'General Papers' of 'Charles Kerrigan'. *Gays Against Imperialism: For Gay Liberation Through National Liberation*, a complex trace interconnected with, not a novelty of, the time that led to now. The queer life is one that moves beyond the structures of political success; so perhaps activists outside the imperial band would search for their own redundancy, aiming for that impossible Utopia where the silent life is no longer the dangerous one, and the mono wouldn't drown out the poly.

Conversations occurring outside the imperial band would always pose a threat to receding Empires who grow fearful of the multitude's sedition — a sedition that the imperial band is called upon to alienate, *then* separate, into privatised, disposable limbs.

> TEBBUTT. [British] 'Home Front' propaganda during the Second World War displayed similar alarm at the seditious possibilities of women's conversation [...] One of the earliest campaigns planned by the Ministry of Information in 1939 was that against 'Careless Talk,' which targeted the destructive role of 'gossiping housewives'. The same patronizing tendency pervaded a speech which A.A. Milne drafted for a Royal Broadcaster in 1939, in which the Queen was [scripted] to speak 'as a wife and mother to other wives and mothers, and as a woman to all other women', which recommended ways of keeping up [Front Line] morale.[40]

---

40. Melanie Tebbutt, *Women's Talk: A Social History of Gossip in Working-class Neighborhoods, 1880-1960*, England: Scolar Press, 1995, p29-30

A.A. Milne's drafted speech for the Queen read

> QUEEN. Men say we gossip. Well, perhaps we do. It is nice sitting cosily with a friend and saying "Did you hear this" and "Did you hear that". But please, please, don't let us gossip now. Don't tell each other what the milkman said — it isn't true; how would the milkman know?' [...] You will help me so much if you remember this; and perhaps it will help you to remember, when you are tempted to spread these rumours ...just say to yourself "The Queen herself asked me not to. She asked me".[41]

She didn't

> TEBBUTT. Although this condescending little missive was never broadcast, it was complimented by the director general for its admirably human touch.[42]

X

Words, like names, are sometimes heavy; like symptoms that hide causes. At times, it was as if our audio recordings were propositional, and Cathal was speaking in fourth person about another life and a former self. In many ways, he was. Homosexual experience could have been considered incongruous with capitalism, when no orientation other than straight had a place. In 2014, when we first met in Cork, it seemed as if some things from those times were repeating, albeit in different ways with different dates and names.

'Bear in mind', Cathal reminded me often, 'we are sitting here in this apartment, drinking beer, and talking politely and respectfully. Thirty years ago, I would have been screaming this at you'.

---

41. Ibid
42. Ibid

Cathal and I had first met at the end of December 2014. A few months before I had emailed the Student Union office of University College Cork, as I knew Charles Kerrigan had been President in 1981. 'Yes, I was Charles Kerrigan,' read the first email from Cathal[43], who was, by chance, a librarian at the same University. In the photocopied photograph, Cathal's head was down — as if muffling his voice — it was for 'National Liberation', not 'Nationalism', I kept reminding myself[44]. When I look at the photocopied photograph, I imagine Cathal shouting — 'Gaze Against Imperialism!', I mishear — which is the right and wonder of any first encounter — prompting the most civic and poetic of questions: 'what did you say?', not 'what did they call you?'

---

43. Note: Cathal is the Irish Language version of Charles.
44. See Cedric J. Robinson, *Black Marxism*, London: The University of North Carolina Press, 2000, p 101: 'Marx came to insist that national liberation was the precondition for proletarian internationalism and simultaneously the destruction of bourgeois economic, political, military, and ideological hegemony. He did not, however, extend this analysis to India, Mexico, or Italy. Engels, on the other hand, tended to recognise and emphasize a counterrevolutionary tendency of national liberation movements, which he had sensed since observing the social upheavals of 1848-49.'

Gaze Against Imperialism

Scenes with Cathal Kerrigan

INT. PHONE CALL - AFTERNOON

KERRIGAN.   So, where to begin?

ROBINSON.   Let's begin with the photocopy of the photograph in the Irish Queer Archive.

KERRIGAN.   The one you emailed?

ROBINSON.   *Gays Against Imperialism.*

KERRIGAN.   Yes.

ROBINSON.   I found it on my second visit in 2014 and didn't really know where to place it. The material I had viewed up to that point seemed to track a conflict between legal reform activism and the social enterprise of the then emerging 'gay scene'. A speech that Davis Norris gave at the Annual General Meeting of the *National Gay Federation* in 1981 exemplified this for me. Were you present at that actually?

KERRIGAN.   No, I was never a member of the *National Gay Federation*. Other people I knew were. What was the speech?

ROBINSON.   'It would be an appalling irony if the net impact of the gay liberation movement was merely to make homosexuality safe for capitalism'. That is the sentence that stayed in my mind at least.

KERRIGAN.   That surprises me, I would have thought of David Norris as a reformist, whose aim was to integrate. *Gays Against Imperialism* meant 'liberation' to mean the overthrow of a system, not reforming it.

ROBINSON.   From what I can gather, I think Norris was referring to the legal reform activism of the *National Gay Federation* perhaps being less popular than commercial enterprises like the discos that catered to the then developing gay scene?

KERRIGAN.   Yes, this was a major issue at the time of the split in the organisation in the late 1970s.

ROBINSON.   But does the phrase, not taken too far out of context, also say something about the international view too?

KERRIGAN.   Well, yes, in fact Dennis Altman published a book in 1982 called *The Homosexualization of America, The Americanization of the Homosexual*, so these issues of capitalism transforming gay liberation into market assimilation were being debated internationally.

ROBINSON.   It seems inevitable to my generation that forms of resistance eventually become assimilated into capital production. With the photocopy, I was fascinated by the slogan *Gays Against Imperialism: for Gay Liberation through National Liberation*. It seemed a striking gesture in a public space in 1982 in Ireland. Not seeing *Gay Liberation* as a 'singular issue', but rather something inseparable from class generally. Liberation *through*, not *over*.

KERRIGAN.   *Through*, yes.

ROBINSON.   Not only implicating recent Irish history and British Imperialism, but something international too. I don't know, maybe I am reading too much into the photocopy, how did this all come about?

KERRIGAN.   *Gays Against Imperialism* came about precisely from the sentiments you expressed in terms of the internationalisation of anti-imperial struggle, and the resonance of Gay Liberation

The reconciliation centre in Glencree has made the it's premises available for the exclusive use of gay people for the weekend 28th-30th November, during which lectures, workshops, discussions and other social activities can be enjoyed.

It has been a long time since the Gay Movement in Ireland, initial meeting at which **all** concerned gay groups and individuals, could together assess and evaluate the effectiveness of their efforts in the past and develop new ideas and relationships for the future, to bring about political and social changes to better the quality of life for gay people in Irish Society.

The Cork Wednesday Night Group have, after meetings and activities over a long period become more and more frustrated and concerned that not only is there no unified national movement for groups on individuals to turn to for support, but also that to turn to the N.G.F. or I.G.R.M. in Dublin for support also means acknowledging and encouraging a split in the Gay Movement which we feel has been a destructive influence on the energy of people inside and outside of those movements.

A great deal is being done within both organisations, but if we are to effectively face the challenges of the future we must develop a stronger sense of unity, we must at the very least talk to each other.

Therefore, we have arranged for the use of the facilities in Glencree to be made available for all of Sunday afternoon to discuss the matters mentioned above. We hope we have the support of the council members of the N.G.F. and I.G.R.M. and other gay groups and individuals to come along on Sunday afternoon to try to build a better working relationship between these groups and a **stronger** unified national movement.

9.11.80

in the 1970s and 1980s. So Máirtín Mac An Ghoill and I had founded this thing called *Gays Against Imperialism* because of Máirtín's personal experience as an activist in Belfast. My experience, on the other hand, was limited. Mine was intellectual and I needed some kind of material basis. That is what Máirtín and myself were trying to work out. We were gay, and we supported national liberation. We were Trotskyists and we had a Marxist analysis. So *Gays Against Imperialism* became the slogan that aligned these two things.

ROBINSON. And that it was liberation *through* National Liberation...

KERRIGAN. ...I can't remember but it was probably Máirtín who first brought that up, that it was for *Gay Liberation through National Liberation*. We spent a lot of time on these slogans and the order of the words is significant. This was one of the things that we found to be very controversial at the time, as most people in the gay movement would immediately distance themselves from us, because we gave importance to the National Liberation struggle.

ROBINSON. National Liberation in the Marxist concept, not national in the blood and soil sense.

KERRIGAN. Anti-imperialism, class and the economic struggle, yes. We said these struggles come first. We were fighting and we fought with people in the left in the Trotskyist and Trade Union movement, and even within Sinn Féin and H-Block Armagh committees, arguing that we needed to be part of all this as gay people because we were openly gay anti-imperialists. As gay Marxists we argued that gays were part of the wider social order.

ROBINSON. Not entirely unreasonable at the time.

KERRIGAN. Yes, but it was also a big fallacy because we actually believed that to be truly liberationist by definition, you could only be so in a liberated society that was class free and egalitarian, and based on a new society. Now of course, what the last 35 years have shown is that no, no, no no. You can be totally integrated as a gay capitalist and as a gay bourgeoisie and a gay member of the First World. And not only that, but you'd be popular. You can be the litmus test for European capitalist democracy, its values and human rights. But that was the statement and we were consciously trying to do that. Máirtín and myself painted the banner in the photocopy on a bed sheet from our bedroom.

ROBINSON. Hahaha, I love that.

KERRIGAN. Well there you go, talk about corporeality. *Gays Against Imperialism* was firmly based and planted on the sheets of our bed.

ROBINSON. So there is a love story here.

KERRIGAN. Hahaha, well. Yes.

ROBINSON. Did you meet through your activism?

KERRIGAN. In the summer of 1980, I was in my office when I was UCC Student Union President and in walks Máirtín. I don't know it yet, but he was in trouble. He had dropped out of college in the 1970s. Actually, a lot of people I met back then had dropped out of university to focus on political activism. Máirtín went to Belfast, lived in squats, got involved in riots, and became the Public Relations Officer for the Relative's Action Committee with Bernadette McAliskey[45].

---

45. See Bernadette McAliskey interviewed on *Firing Line with William F. Buckley Jr.: The Irish Problem*, 25.03.79. 'If you continue to talk in terms of Catholic and Protestant, certainly from the beginning of Northern Ireland, there was the Unionist Government Party, which was Protestant, and there was the opposition party, the Nationalist Party, which was Catholic. The main problem was that both were conservative.' https://www.youtube.com/watch?v=FFUKV5_EwdA (Last accessed 08.04.18) For McAliskey's views on protest and post-Fordism see 26:44-32:57

INT. PHONE CALL - AFTERNOON   60.

ROBINSON. Also known by her maiden name, Bernadette Devlin? The youngest MP elected to the British Parliament in the 60s?

KERRIGAN. Yes.

ROBINSON. I still haven't seen Leila Doolan's documentary about McAliskey. I heard Doolan describe the Irish State as a kind of post-colonial adolescent.

KERRIGAN. McAliskey went out of her way to support *Gays Against Imperialism*, and made a special effort to be the lead speaker for our launch in 1982. She had survived an assassination attempt at the hands of Ulster loyalists in 1981, she was very strong, Máirtín knew her very well. When I met him I think he had begun to experience burn out. In 1979 his friends suggested that he needed time out from the struggle up in the North. His friend in Cork offered him some help, so he came down and found a bedsit. So we started to talk and something sparked, I don't know, how does one explain these situations. You know what I mean?

ROBINSON. I do.

KERRIGAN. Hahaha, good, so I mentioned in our conversation that the *Cork Gay Collective* have this British Theatre group coming over to do a performance at the weekend, and invited him to go. Not long after we decided we needed to move in together. This is a huge transformation; he hugely transforms my life over the next few months.

ROBINSON. In political terms?

KERRIGAN. Well to be truthful, yes. I end up leading demos, attending Dublin H-Block Armagh committees, being involved with the Students Against H-Block Armagh. So all of that was transformational. That's why when my term finishes with the student union Máirtín said, 'let's move.' So he moved to Dublin and a week later I follow him, and that's how I end up there.

INT. PHONE CALL – AFTERNOON

ROBINSON.   OK, so to begin again, the picture on the photocopy was taken not long after that, and the banner was made on your bed sheets.

KERRIGAN.   This was Máirtín's drawing, as I couldn't do that. We don't have a word for gay 'as Gaeilge' or at least we didn't know it, so Máirtín was trying to make it up as we went along. That is me, in the cap, with my head down for some reason. This guy here was *National Gay Federation*, lovely guy, but totally not involved, and we can see from his suit and tie that he is not involving himself with us. But look at these guys, *Fair Treatment for Gay Teacher.* It seems so ahead of its time.

ROBINSON.   Incidentally, the figure of the 'gay teacher' is very prevalent in films at the time, such as *Nighthawks* from 1981, and *Coming Out*[46] from 1989, or even *Mädchen in Uniform* decades earlier.

KERRIGAN.   It's not for gay teachers in general though. It's about a specific teacher?

ROBINSON.   Yes, I think it was a protest about a lesbian teacher in Belgium, Eliane Morissens, who spoke about her sexuality

---

46. See the final word uttered by actor Mathias Freihof at the end of the film Coming Out, 1989, the first and only DDR film dealing explicitly with homosexual experience. It premiered in East Berlin on the 9th November 1989, the same day the Berlin Wall Fell. The film follows high school teacher Phillip in the final days of the DDR. Phillip's 'I' emerges defiant from the socialist 'we', yet his will to power takes on an altogether different type of synchronicity with the historical accident of the parallel event: the premiere and the fall. Coming out and falling down, this last word was delivered at the end of a silent protest in response to Phillip's class being observed by school 'officials'. Refusing to teach by saying nothing, he looks out of the window, into an East Berlin where the wall is about to fall. The former oppression would soon give rise to a new economic liberty. When shouted at by the school Principal to do something, Phillip ends his silent protest by standing up in front the class, knowingly saying "Ja!".

INT. PHONE CALL – AFTERNOON

                on television, and was banned from teaching in 1980. Her appeal didn't get heard until around a year later in 1981. She eventually went on hunger strike and there was a protest in The Hague on January 23, 1982.

KERRIGAN.   That is ringing a bell.

ROBINSON.   Might it have been a simultaneous protest with the one *Gays Against Imperialism* was photographed at?

KERRIGAN.   Ah, that parallel with the hunger strike definitely would have caught our attention. It was so long ago, I can't remember exact dates, but it was indeed a protest at the firing of Eliane Morissens. I can't remember, but do you know what happened in that case in the end?

ROBINSON.   A commission declared that her dismissal was a 'proportional' measure and her case was declared inadmissible.[47] I don't know what happened after that. Cases like that sadly disappear.

KERRIGAN.   It's a pity that her case disappeared, I suppose that's the importance of queer archives. So the photograph was taken at the Belgian embassy in Dublin then. Yes. It was a *National Gay Federation* organized protest probably after there was an international call for solidarity. It must have been early in 1982, so the photograph was probably taken in February that year. I can't remember the photographer though. I don't have the original so it must have been given to me as a photocopy, as that was the quickest way to copy pictures then, and that is what is in the archive. Now, bear in mind, many of the other

---

47.   *Yearbook of the European Convention of Human Rights*, Dordrecht: Martinus Nijhoff Publishers, 1988, p 41 – 45. A statement by Eliane Morissens read: 'Then people said, though unfortunately this was never stated in writing, that it was unthinkable that a homosexual woman should be put in charge of a school with 1,000 girls. I find that rather amusing! There are at present two men in charge of the school; I don't know whether that doesn't make the risk all the greater'

people there, if you were to talk to them, would say 'well that was typical of Cathal and Máirtín and their crowd because there was only ever three or four of them.' They would tell you that 'Cathal and Máirtín would turn up with their banner and it would look like it was their protest, when in fact no one else in the protest would support our views.'

ROBINSON. The *Gays Against Imperialism* banner was the subject of the photographer not the protest.

KERRIGAN. Yes. Public relations.

ROBINSON. To my mind, there *is* an imperialism at play in the case of Eliane Morissens, but would you agree with the perception of the others, who as you say, would imply that you kind of crashed the protest?

KERRIGAN. Well I'd have to, because it *was* what we did. We were very confrontational. We were a very small group of people. Tiny group of people actually, you could count us on the fingers of one hand really. We found ourselves in situations where our ideological connectivity was to people on the broader left.

ROBINSON. In Ireland or beyond Ireland too?

KERRIGAN. Well both, but particularly in Ireland, we were situated in Ireland, and in the situation where we all identified as left wing.

ROBINSON. Before identifying as homosexual you were left wing in the sense of your past?

KERRIGAN. Well it's very hard to say. One would have to start going through the motivations of each individual, but certainly in general yes and in my case yes. I mean I came out of a Social Democratic background in Ireland. My paternal grandfather in Cork was one of the founders of the Irish Transport and General Worker Union.

ROBINSON. Hard-core worker politics, which must have come at a cost?

INT. PHONE CALL – AFTERNOON

KERRIGAN. Yes. When he was a shop steward he led a strike that took place in Cork before the 1913 strike in Dublin. It failed and he was blacklisted. His sons, my father and his brothers, were all involved in Labour Party Trade Union politics in the 1940s, 50s and 60s. So when I came of age, having been born in 1955, I was born into a family with a very strong identification with Labour. It wouldn't have been Marxist. It was Social Democratic. The big symbol for us in my family household was Harold Wilson, who was a Labour Party leader who was in *power* in Britain. That was a big thing to people in my family. They were always out of power. Fianna Fáil had power, Fine Gael had power, and they were the two big dominant parties. Fianna Fáil had used DeVelara's famous comment "Labour Must Wait". Fianna Fáil had stolen the Labour Party's style of clothing, the Trade Unionists, The Syndicalist, the Left Wing. The organized Labour, Social Democratic voice was a minority that had been demonized by the 1950s in Ireland. My father had been labelled as an atheist, even though he was a believing Catholic on a personal level. So all of this awful stuff happened before I was born.

ROBINSON. So a political urgency was always felt through your family?

KERRIGAN. Absolutely. In fact, by the time I became politically aware I felt more radical than my father. He was a Labour Party Parliamentarian from 1973 until 1979 when he died, and was Lord Mayor of Cork from 1973 – 1974. I identified with things that, looking back now, are dreadful to think of. Cultural Revolution, all of that was the bee's-knees. It was where I wanted to be. It is awful to think of now, particularly as I did get to visit China in the 21st Century, and began to really realize the implications of the Maoist Cultural Revolution in terms of its barbarity and viciousness. But as a 15 year old in Cork, Ireland, in 1970, you know...

ROBINSON. Of course, it is dreadful to think of now, but there wasn't the global digital awareness as we have now. You had to actively search or nothing came. Everything now is basically delivered and manipulated through social media.

KERRIGAN. Oh yeah, then it was very hard to get information. This active searching was one of the simple things I shared with other people. In the 1990s I worked with a guy from England and who had a Trotskyist background. We both shared the same story, of being teenagers in 1970 writing to the Chinese Embassy and the Soviet Embassy, and getting back these packages about the life of Lenin. The thing to remember is the Maoists actually existed in Ireland, and they were based, ironically enough, in Trinity College Dublin. That great bastion of privilege. They became very famous and the media treated them as an oddity and put them on television. They were on the *Late Late Show* and Gay Byrne interviewed this guy who was a politics student from Trinity who was the leader of the Irish Maoists. Of course, the whole absurdity was that these were children of the privileged, a bit like the RAF in Germany. Children of the most privileged being presented on the *Late Late Show* to the parents and the children of the underprivileged.[48]

ROBINSON. The masses.

KERRIGAN. The masses: the people who had to work for a living. It was the absurdity that not alone did they have every privilege thrown at them, but they were rejecting it all to declare that everything was wrong and that we needed a revolution. What they thought we needed was to be going around wearing the same clothes etc.

ROBINSON. And did this 'searching' overlap with the beginnings of the

---

48. See *Nusight*, May 1970, a monthly Irish News magazine edited by Vincent Browne: 'Sociologically the student Maoists are explicable as an altogether extreme reaction by young idealists to a society that has not solved the problems that beset its people. That young people can take up with such conviction a philosophy that bears little relation to their own experience, or indeed to Irish experience generally, indicates precisely the extraordinary lack of faith among the younger generation in the norms and values of contemporary Western society.' https://www.marxists.org/history/erol/ireland/maoists.pdf (Last accessed 09.03.15)

INT. PHONE CALL – AFTERNOON

                    Gay Rights Movement for you around 1975 or was this too early?

KERRIGAN.   No this was around 1970, so I was still a teenager at this stage, and to answer your question, before I became consciously gay. At this stage I was just 15, I had gone through puberty and was becoming aware of a sexual impulse through masturbation and masturbatory images, and fancying other guys at school, you know, these beautiful guys. At the time all that was still OK. The big change came around 1971, when I was 16 and went into a downward spin. Because suddenly I became aware that I was queer and perceived negatively in the culture at the time, so I became very negative in return. I was deeply religious and reading St. John of The Cross, which has a masochistic sexual kind of thing. On a simple level, to be very crude, I started masturbating and I just instinctively knew that this was too pleasurable to be good. I knew the minute I told the priest he would tell me it was bad for me...

ROBINSON.   ...you and more than half of Ireland at the time...

KERRIGAN.   ...So I adopted an avoidance strategy. I didn't confess it in confession. So when you ask, were we left wing before being *Gays Against Imperialism*, the answer is yes, I was. But we all went through the trauma of being sexual *and* homosexual in a society that was totally opposed to sexuality.

ROBINSON.   When you were a teenager, were you aware that homosexual acts between males were at that time illegal?

KERRIGAN.   Oh absolutely, but to be honest you didn't see people being dragged to prison, so it was more of a social thing for me. I knew at this stage as I had crushes on people at school. I mean I did have friends in school. I was fucked up but I wasn't totally stupid, so I managed to make friends with the people I fancied. You didn't pay too much attention to legal matters and we didn't have the level of knowledge that young people have now.

ROBINSON. Did *Gays Against Imperialism* attach at all to the legal reform campaign of Mary Robinson and David Norris?

KERRIGAN. No, in fact we totally disagreed with it and saw it as a waste of time.

ROBINSON. That surprises me...

KERRIGAN. ...Well, we believed politically that you needed to connect with people and have a social activism that changes society. We thought that legal reform was just upper middle class, intellectual and bourgeois. For us it was about changing attitudes, you don't change the laws because the laws are the problem, and it is in people's minds that social progress happens. So we were opposed to David Norris's campaign because we saw it as middle class, intellectual, narcissistic masturbation. You might change the law but it was not going to change anything on the streets.

ROBINSON. You saw it as centrist?

KERRIGAN. We were speaking from the left, as Marxists wanting actual change, but realizing that the economic structures create the class structures.

ROBINSON. The whole notion of the 'worker' as the only counter to capitalism is a much more complex topic now than ever, especially in terms of identifying ways to alter social infrastructure.

KERRIGAN. Yes, and that is the problem. It has not changed. My generation failed abysmally.

ROBINSON. Well, don't absolve the subsequent generations either.

KERRIGAN. We altered a lot. We altered Ireland majorly; we went from an Ireland where sex was not talked about to where gays and lesbians are in discussion, we altered the situation for families and for single parents, we altered things for women, for youth, but we did not change the fundamental — the

INT. PHONE CALL – AFTERNOON

economic structure. And that is not just true for Ireland, it is true for my generation across the whole world.

ROBINSON. This is then about how people behave in positions of power. Or rather, how people are corrupted by *traditions* of power.

KERRIGAN. The Clintons, for instance, in a way, are core to this, and this is going to come up again with Hillary next year. This is my generation. We all failed in the economic struggle. Capitalism has performed double somersaults and became far cleverer than we ever thought. Capitalism has survived crises and has more importantly turned our anti-capitalist, revolutionary ideas into corporate and financial support structures.

ROBINSON. In terms of being against the singular issue of gay legal reform from a Marxist position, I understand, but by foregrounding 'National Liberation', was there an impression, even a false one, that *Gays Against Imperialism* was directly supporting paramilitary activity?

KERRIGAN. Yes, but we were not directly involved in the IRA, and we didn't stand by a lot of what they did.

ROBINSON. How did you respond?

KERRIGAN. I would have said I support their right to fight, their right to struggle.

ROBINSON. That is open to misrepresentation.

KERRIGAN. We would be as fuzzy as necessary. We were rather *Jesuitical,* if I may use that phrase. Bernadette McAliskey and other people would be interviewed on television as *Provo* sympathizers when, under Section 31 of the Broadcasting Censorship Act, the media couldn't interview anyone from Sinn Féin. Many people held the position that they would support people's right to fight against oppression. They would not condemn people, while they were not supporting everything they did.

ROBINSON. You sent me a scan of a photograph from your personal archive where you were at a protest holding up a banner, '*Gay's Against H-Block Armagh*'. Was it in Derry or somewhere?

KERRIGAN. It was in Dublin, and it was Máirtín and myself again. In fact it was only Máirtín and myself then. It was a miserable and wet day in Dublin. I think it was just before Bobby Sands died, around April 1981. If you look closely, I am wearing sneakers and they are drenched. Eamonn O'Dwyer was a photographer who documented all of these radical movements. We knew him personally and he was very supportive of us. By the time we were let in, we were no longer with our friends. There was suddenly this 50-meter gap between us and the people behind. Eamonn wanted to photograph us and I remember him saying, 'Just stop, just stop. Stand!' He waited until the people caught up so when you look at the photograph you can see people behind us.

ROBINSON. So it was a staged scene?

KERRIGAN. It was a staged photograph. Actually he had to keep us waiting a good two minutes to get those people behind us.

ROBINSON. So the *Gays Against H-Block Armagh* banner was in 1981, one year before the 1982 *Gay's Against Imperialism* banner?

KERRIGAN. Yes, oh absolutely. That was a forerunner. It was six months after the *H-Block Armagh* protest that we were living in Dublin. But then the 1982 *Gays Against Imperialism* began to travel. Tarlagh O'Neill was a gay activist in Derry who approached us as he had just heard about our H-Block Armagh banner at the Dublin protest. Tarlagh invited us to Derry and we went there on an anniversary of the Bloody Sunday protest.

So we went to Derry to Tarlagh and there were all of these gay guys in the Bogside, and they were just so overjoyed at the idea of a gay banner at a Republican demonstration. They were in that community, they were supportive of the struggle, they were part of it, but they were not visible. We

INT. PHONE CALL - AFTERNOON   72.

brought our banner and they all marched. I could not believe it, there were 15 people marching with us. Máirtín and myself were the only outsiders. All of the rest were from Derry. So that was an important moment.

ROBINSON.   Did the *Gays Against Imperialism* banner get seen in the North?

KERRIGAN.   Another Tarlagh, Tarlagh Mac Niallais in Belfast made contact with us as he was very much involved in anti-imperialism activism, and he made the *Belfast Gays Against Imperialism* banner a year later in 1983.

ROBINSON.   So in terms of the historical pace, *Gays Against H-Block Armagh* and *Gays Against Imperialism*, on a surface reading, would have had Republican implications for people at the time, so people would distance themselves.

KERRIGAN.   Yes, but people in Cork who were involved with left politics were very supportive of Máirtín and myself. Part of all this is that we would not have gone on without their support. We were getting no support really from the Gay Movement, whose position was that it is 'bad enough we are gay, now Cathal and his gang want to associate us with *Provo* lunatics'.

ROBINSON.   What about Sinn Féin and groups who were both North and South of the border?

KERRIGAN.   Even within the H-Block Armagh Campaigns there was lots of different divisions, prejudices and pressures. At the time, Sinn Féin was very conservative and narrow, and very Catholic. I mean we had arguments in the H-Block Armagh campaign about people saying the Rosary as part of a demonstration. In Dublin Sinn Féin controlled, in Cork, they didn't. So people like Alan Bruce and Jim Lane could overrule Sinn Féin, so we wouldn't say the Rosary. People could say it privately, but it would not have a public moment.

In terms of Máirtín and myself, they were interested in having everyone against H-Block Armagh, something that was representative of society; women against, nurses against,

INT. PHONE CALL – AFTERNOON

gays against etc. We started in Cork with the support of this all-inclusive Left, then we got to Dublin with the *Gays Against H-Block Armagh* banner and one year later, in February 1982, the *Gays Against Imperialism: For Gay Liberation through National Liberation* banner was photographed at the Belgian embassy.

Grif

Université des Femmes

Bulletin 6

INFORMATIONS GENERALES

"SOS VIOL" A BESOIN DE VOS TEMOIGNAGES

L'association "SOS VIOL" de Bruxelles demande aux femmes qui ont subi une agression sexuelle (viol ou tentative de viol), d'en parler anonymement en répondant au questionnaire qu'elle a mis sur pied.

En effet, active depuis quatre ans, l'ASBL se propose aujourd'hui pour objectif, en donnant la parole aux femmes, de lutter contre le viol et de modifier les textes de loi qui régissent le fonctionnement de la justice.

Il est indispensable que les femmes sortent de leur silence pour raconter l'agression qu'elles ont subie, pour réfuter les préjugés traditionnels, rechercher les vraies causes d'un phénomène si répandu et préparer de nouvelles solutions.

Face au viol, les femmes sont solidaires pour revendiquer le droit à l'intégrité de leur corps et à l'expression de leurs désirs. En réalisant ce questionnaire, l'association offre aux femmes l'occasion d'exprimer leur solidarité.

Leurs réponses permettront à l'ASBL de baser son travail sur des faits précis et des statistiques valables.

Le questionnaire peut être obtenu gratuitement sur simple demande à

SOS VIOL
place Quételet, 1a
1030 Bruxelles
tél. 219.28.02 de 10 à 17 h.

COMITE DE SOUTIEN A ELIANE MORISSENS

Eliane MORISSENS, enseignante dans une école provinciale du Hainaut, a été frappée d'interdiction professionnelle pour avoir participé, le 28 octobre 1980, à une émission de télévision sur l'homosexualité où elle a témoigné à visage découvert.

Cette décision était confirmée le 19 décembre 1980 par la Députation Permanente du Hainaut qui décidait alors officiellement de la suspendre de ses fonctions d'enseignante. Eliane Morissens a immédiatement interjeté appel. Ce n'est pourtant que le ... 27 novembre 1981 qu'elle a été appelée à comparaître devant la commission d'appel. Depuis, elle attend toujours la décision finale de la Députation Permanente.

Ne pouvant pas accepter la mesure arbitraire et contraire au droit à l'existence et à l'expression des diversités, qui la frappe, ayant attendu plus qu'il n'est tolérable, que l'on statue définitivement sur son sort, <u>Eliane Morissens a décidé de commencer le lundi 18 janvier au matin une grève de la faim illimitée</u> pour obtenir sa réintégration.

Une nouvelle Députation Permanente est en place. Il lui est possible de statuer rapidement. Il lui est possible de casser la décision prise par la Députation précédente et de réintégrer Eliane Morissens dans ses fonctions et au poste qu'elle occupait avant d'apparaître à la télévision, seule mesure acceptable car toute autre équivaudrait à reconnaître l'existence d'un délit d'homosexualité ou d'expression.

Nous avons besoin de votre aide pour que cette lutte aboutisse enfin rapidement. L'issue de cette grève de la faim dépend de ce que vous pourrez faire.

Il faut constituer des comités de soutien dans chaque ville et chaque village de la province et en dehors. Contactez-nous pour nous indiquer vos disponibilités. N'hésitez pas à prendre des initiatives.

Nous nous permettons aussi, en toute franchise et sans fausse pudeur, de vous signaler que cette action entraîne de nombreux frais qu'Eliane ne peut assumer seule. Nous demandons donc à chacun(e) de contribuer financièrement dès maintenant aux frais de cette campagne. Le temps est court. Faites un effort pour répondre très rapidement. Merci.

Comité de soutien à Eliane MORISSENS
rue du Petit Moulin 2 - 6520 FELUY
tél. (067) 87.72.21   Soutien financier : compte n°
                       068.0854260.08 - mention : action
ou à Bruxelles   MORISSENS
Rue du Prince Royal 25 - 1050 Bruxelles
tél. (02) 512.64.04

[TRANSLATION]

GENERAL INFORMATION

SOS VIOL NEEDS YOUR TESTIMONIES

The Brussel-based SOS VIOL organisation is asking women who got sexually assaulted (rape or attempted rape) to talk about it anonymously by answering the questionnaire they have prepared.

Active for the last four years, the ASBL today pursues the objective of empowering women to speak, fighting against rape and modifying legislation that governs the functioning of justice.

It is essential that women start to speak out in order to describe the assaults they have endured and to fight traditional prejudices, looking for the real causes of such a widespread phenomena and to prepare new solutions.

Solidarity amongst women against rape is needed in order to claim for their bodies the right for integrity and for the expression of their desires. By creating this questionnaire, the organisation is giving women the chance to express their solidarity.

Their answers will help the ASBL to base its work on precise facts and reliable statistical information.

Ask for a free questionnaire at:

SOS VIOL
Place Quételet, 1a
1030 BRUXELLES
Tel. 219.28.02 from 10 a.m. to 5 p.m.

SUPPORT COMMITTEE FOR ELIANE MORISSENS

Eliane MORISSENS, teacher at a provincial school of Hainaut, got banned from teaching after participating in an October 28th 1980 TV show about homosexuality where she talked openly.

On December 19th 1980, this decision was confirmed by the Provincial Standing Committee of the Hainaut council who officially decided to suspend her from teaching. Eliane Morissens immediately appealed. It was only on November 27th 1981 that she was called in to appear and appeal before the board. She has been waiting for the final decision of the Hainut Council ever since.

Since she cannot accept the arbitrary measures taken against her, which is contrary to the right to exist and the expression of diversity, and having waited for so long is not acceptable for a final decision to be taken, <u>Eliane Morissens has now decided to go on an unlimited hunger strike starting on Monday, January 18th in the morning</u>, in order to obtain her job back.

A new Provincial Standing Committee is now in charge and should be able to reach a quicker decision. It should be able to quash the decision taken by the former Council and reinstate Eliane MORISSENS in the function and the job she was previously assigned to before appearing on television. It is the only acceptable measure, any other would be to recognise the expression of homosexuality as an offence.

We need your help to end this fight quickly. The continuation of that hunger strike depends on what you can do.

Support committees have to be created in every city and every village of the province and beyond. Contact us to indicate your availabilities. Don't hesitate to take initiatives.

Quite frankly and simply put, we should also like to inform you that this direct action requires a certain amount of costs that Eliane cannot cope with unaided. We ask everyone now to contribute financially to the campaign costs. We don't have much time. Make an effort to respond rapidly. Thank you.

Support Committee to Eliane MORISSENS
rue du petit moulin 2 - 6520 FELUY
tel. (02) 512.64.04   Financial support : account n°
                           ~~068.0854260.08~~ reference: action
or in Brussels   MORISSENS

Rue du Prince Royal 25 - 1050 Bruxelles
tel. (02) 512.64.04

INT. LIBRARY - MORNING

KERRIGAN. These seven struts were the conceptual framework in 1982 for *Gays Against Imperialism: For Gay liberation through National Liberation* — the portmanteau name bringing together these seven supports in a *hard, gem-like flame* — the slogan intended to make the concept more explicit and at the same time provocative — the *'through'* focusing attention on the sequencing while suggesting a penetrative dynamic!

1. There was the Marxism of the 1960s New Left based on the humanism of Marx's Economic & Philosophical Manuscripts.

2. There was the existentialism of Satre — Being & Nothingness — read for philosophy at university, shocking me out of my Catholic romantic reverie with its stark declaration that our existence only becomes a life when we make choices.

3. There was the Women's Liberation Movement, which focused attention on the hidden role women had played in the early 20th century struggles, highlighted by the works of revolutionaries such as Alexandra Kollontai and Emma Goldman. Feminism gave us the analytical tools with which to deconstruct the Leviathan of — anatomy — gender — roles — orientation — sexuality.

4. There were the European and American war children of 1945–1960 discovering that they were the new promised

leisure class, having the wealth and the technology to allow all to live like aristocrats of the Roman Empire and find fun and fulfillment in just enjoying life. I was born in 1955 and so as a baby-boomer lived my life in the bubble of the longest continuous economic boom under capitalism (until it crashed in 2008) — allowing me to spend my time fighting against this very system!

5. There was the anti-imperialist struggle feeding energetic idealism into the world after the Second World War right into the 1980s — Che Guevara was then still an inspiring symbol of these struggles for independence and autonomy by peoples across the globe.

6. There was the spirit of Neo-Platonism — The Perennial Philosophy — as represented by the poetry of William Blake, Walt Whitman and Allen Ginsberg — a balancing element to the barrenness of materialism, it showed a way to spontaneous joy and a new, alternative spirituality helping create solidarity and cementing community.

7. There was the work and life of Jean Genet. An ideological snake-charmer who fascinated by refusing all definitions and praise. Like a Daoist sage making explicit that the only certainty was change. He refused the role of prophet and instead wore a mask— like Anonymous — like Guy Fawkes in "V for Vendetta" — Genet's writing declared to me: 'That we must struggle to free ourselves from the restraints imposed on us and if we should succeed immediately start fighting against any new restraints imposed by that successful struggle'.

It wasn't until 1987 in London that I saw Genet's play *The Balcony*, with Irish actor Gerard Murphy. It blew my mind. The various endings I take to be his protean refusal of fixture but also his swinging from optimistic to pessimistic views of revolutionary outcomes.

The launch of *Gays Against Imperialism* in 1982 was my perfectly balanced moment when I clutched the strings of all seven balloons at once and dreamed of floating off like the boy in the drawing. But it didn't take off. I felt guilt as my presentation had fallen flat.

If success comes on an isolated basis where the focus is solely on singular issue politics, such as gay rights, then many of those whose attitudes are changed will remain unchanged in their attitudes on other social issues. This disappointment gives rise to my dismay when I find myself speaking with gay conservatives, gay capitalists and others.

In the summer of 1992 I'd arrived weary in Amsterdam — burnout driving me to seek refuge from a decade and a half struggle with left politics in Ireland. My friend Uta was teaching me Dutch at the same time as a three-month sublet I had found was coming to an end. I was putting up notices seeking accommodation and she had suggested I draft a text in Dutch and she would correct it. She sounded puzzled as she read *homo Ier zoekt*. 'Why do you say 'gay Irishman' ? she asked. When I explained that I didn't want confrontation after I'd arrived or moved in that someone has an issue with my being gay, she said, 'Cathal, this is Amsterdam — if they have an issue with you being gay — that's exactly it — it's they who have a problem not you!'

The knowledge that I was living in a place where homophobia was seen as the problem and represented only a minority was the oxygen that allowed me to breathe, relax and feel at home in Amsterdam for the next seven years. I left Amsterdam in 1999 just as Pim Fortuyn was launching his new right party; it proved so phenomenally successful that within 12 months it was polling over 20%. It looked likely that after the general election in 2001, Fortuyn was due to be kingmaker of the next Dutch government. While articulating his right wing xenophobic, economic and cultural views, Fortuyn was open about his homosexuality; this allowed his supporters to contest accusations that they were intolerant in their policies and politics. Sure, didn't they follow an openly gay leader?

Press Release   **Preas Ráitea**

Students' Union,
University College,
Cork.

FOR IMMEDIATE USE

U.C.C. GAY SOC.

The Joint Board of UCC at its meeting on Wednesday (13/5/1981) decided merely to "note" the copious correspondence querying its decision not to grant recognition to the Gay Society. Last January the Joint Board refused to grant recognition to the Gay Soc. and would not discuss its reasons for doing so. Since then letters demanding that the Joint Board give its reasons have come from the College Chaplains, the Arts Faculty Staff-Student Committee, the Socialist Society, Queens University S.U., UCD S.U., Union of Students in Ireland, Cork Gay Collective, Irish Gay Rights Movement, other groups and many individuals.

The Gay Soc. has operated for the past six months with the support of the Students' Union. It has held meetings in conjunction with other societies (e.g., Socialist Society, Cogito Soc.) and contributed to the general life of College, with its own craft in the Boat Race during College Week.

The recent decision of the Executive Committee of IFUT not to put a motion on Gay Rights to the ICTU Annual Congress and the UCC Joint Board's continued refusal to give its reasons for banning the Gay Soc. are both regrettable, as silent encouragement of prejudice.

CHARLES KERRIGAN
General Secretary, S.U.

15 May, 1981.

Gay Republicans for Trump in 2016; prominent gays supporting Marine Le Pen and the Front National in the 2017 French presidential race; vocal gay support for Brexit and Theresa May's Conservative Party in Britain; more visible expressions of the co-existence of an open and increasingly confident gay population with economic and racist reactionary views surfacing in online dating sites as *no Asians, no blacks, etc; and* gay male surrogacy arguments that these two-income middle-class households could provide much better for children than lower income heterosexual single-parent households.

These developments have knocked me off kilter and challenged me to review my politics — they have undermined my confidence in my political analysis.

The Ireland I returned to in 1999 was totally changed. The Celtic Tiger boom was in full flow. But also social attitudes had changed dramatically with the legalisation of homosexuality in 1993 and subsequent equality legislation. When I moved back to Cork in 2003 and took up work in the university library, I was amazed to discover that the student Gay Society had been voted the most popular student society on campus. I was put in contact with the Gay Society as they were interested in hearing about its initial founding and the efforts I made in making it possible in the early 80s. I was dumbstruck when I discovered the auditor and secretary were also officers in Young Fine Gael. Not only that, they took it for granted that this was so!

This is the paradox of fighting prejudice: to succeed one must change the attitudes and views of the homophobes and in the process win over the whole population. Being successful means eliminating homophobia completely and doing away with the need for struggle. Doing away with the existence of gay organizations entirely. We used to joke that we were fighting to make ourselves redundant.

So I found myself sitting with Young Fine Gaeler's, who saw no contradiction whatsoever between their LGBTQ lives and Christian Democratic politics. They were in turn

INT. LIBRARY - MORNING

>mystified by my amazement, and found absurd my perspective that their conservative economic and political views conflicted with their gay rights stance. In reality they were a microcosm of what happened to LGBTQ politics as we entered the 21st century.

INT. GAY BAR - NIGHT

ROBINSON. When we ended our phone call, what I understood was there was a disruptive element to your politics, rather focused on people's mind-sets than the back rooms of state bureaucracy and single issue politics.

KERRIGAN. Yes, street politics.

ROBINSON. I then began to think that, actually, no sincere political imagination in 1981 could have ignored the situation in the North? Because at the level of everyday life, beyond political identity, at the end of the day, the Troubles were a left over from a civil war that few wanted.

KERRIGAN. Nobody ever wants a civil war, and it is so complex because civil war can turn brother against sister, sister against brother. It turns father against daughter, son against mother. It turns neighbour against neighbour. It is a viciously divisive thing and the problem is that these people know each other inside out. If you're fighting a foreign enemy you've got the support of your own. In civil war it's your own you're fighting, who know where you go, and who know where the hideouts might be. People who know how you think. And it very rapidly becomes vicious and awful. And that's what happened throughout Irish history.

ROBINSON. But what about this reductive mind-set equating all discussions of Northern Ireland with paramilitary activity? Was that used to denounce you politically?

INT. GAY BAR – NIGHT

KERRIGAN.   There is a story about David Norris and me which took place in 1982. It was in the *Hirschfeld Centre*, you've heard of it.

ROBINSON.   The first gay centre in Dublin, in Temple Bar, which was burned down?

KERRIGAN.   Yes, and the *National Gay Federation* administration offices were there and it was also used as a kind of post 'drop off' point. From the best of my recollection this happened on a Saturday morning, at, or around, lunch hour.

ROBINSON.   OK.

KERRIGAN.   So I had picked up whatever it was I needed, and was just sitting around laughing with some other guys I knew. They were having a meeting so I was heading out. Of course, as usual, I got delayed chatting. Then suddenly Davis Norris storms in. Remember, it was *his* organisation, *his* premises, *his* politics and *his* committee meeting. He and I didn't get on. As such, we weren't friends. So he strides in the room, sees me joking with the others, and goes to the top of the table. I say to the others that I am going to get out of their way so the meeting can go on. I was trying to get out as quickly as possible. As I was putting my hand on the door to leave the room, I hear Norris shout: 'You, Charles Kerrigan.' I say: 'What David?' and he says 'You are a provo lover, and you are friends with people who want to murder me. I have received death threats from the Provo IRA who say they are going to kill me because I am not an Irish citizen.' I said to him it was the first I have ever heard of it. It sounded like absolute nonsense so I asked for proof.

ROBINSON.   Wait, you actually saw the death threat?

KERRIGAN.   He said he didn't have it there, and in the end never produced it. I had no proof.

ROBINSON.   Whoa... I am not sure what to say, it seems so serious and petty at the same time.

KERRIGAN. That was the lunacy of the times. Crazy when I think back on it. I realise this all probably sounds absurd to you, but it's the way micro politics works. David Norris, *the leader,* declared me as 'provo loving' in front of these other gay community leaders.

ROBINSON. So you felt isolated by it?

KERRIGAN. There was certainly a political effect to it, and Máirtín and I were absolutely furious. So what we did was, we contacted somebody in Sinn Féin, and they said to leave it with them. So we did. We heard nothing for three months and then this person came back to us and said something like, 'I want you to quote authoritatively that your request has been presented to the Army Council of the IRA. They have heard the claim made by David Norris and want to state categorically that they have never ever sanctioned a death threat against him, they never would, in fact they have a policy in support of Gay Rights.'

The weirdest thing about this policy is that it was passed by the Army Council of the IRA, which was more radical, Marxist and left wing than Sinn Féin, who didn't have a pro-gay policy back then. The IRA did. It all sounds absurd now, I know, but what Norris in fact had done was denounce me as what he and members of the Workers Party used to call *green fascists.*

ROBINSON. I don't know what that means?

KERRIGAN. The purpose in calling us green fascists was to undermine our international credibility, by saying we were not progressive and socialist, but that we were like fascist thugs. We weren't.

ROBINSON. So Máirtín's experiences in the North challenged your political background in the South, and you had to deal with that.

INT. GAY BAR – NIGHT

KERRIGAN. My whole politics then changed. You could query that.

ROBINSON. I wouldn't on many levels. I think interpersonal experience is a much better entry to political imagination than the professionalized search for party power. Decadent lobbyist you are not, right?

KERRIGAN. Hahaha, no...

ROBINSON. ...so you were...

KERRIGAN. ...Going north, even just physically, and seeing the north, talking to people there, relating to them, finding them very intelligent, articulate people...

ROBINSON. That sounds patronising. Was it that culturally different?

KERRIGAN. It was a very divisive border in the 1980s. I actually found that the activists I met in the North had a just cause living with the feeling that we had betrayed them in the South. Just to list all the pogroms against Catholics in the North over the decades exposes the level of hypocrisy of us in the South who refused to listen.

ROBINSON. How people behave with power again. Isn't it astounding that my generation grew up with the results of the Good Friday Agreement? So generally speaking for me it was religious identification that polarized the North, how ignorant is that.

KERRIGAN. When I was 15 in 1970 there were already riots in the North. The Orange state was trying to crush the protests of the civil rights movement with Ian Paisley in the background. Then, there were pogroms, like I said. People were being beaten up, cars were burning in the streets, and people were being burned out by Protestant and loyalist gangs. So what happened is that it started a movement down here, a kind soft Republicanism.

ROBINSON. Soft?

KERRIGAN.   Like a *Human Interest* story.

ROBINSON.   I'm not following?

KERRIGAN.   Well, the idea would be that the South would take children from the North and at least give them a break during the summer. Bringing them down for holiday camps in the South. There was one set up by a guy here in Cork, and I always remember that the local tabloid in Cork, the *Evening Echo*, had a headline that showed it all. 'Northern Children Stealing Sweets From Shop' or something. I mean, what is going on there? There are so many subtexts in that headline?

ROBINSON.   Creating fear?

KERRIGAN.   By today's standards you'd say it's outrageous, you know, but that's what it was like at the time. There was a huge, you know, habit of people covering their ...

ROBINSON.   Fear?

KERRIGAN.   Fear, yes, but also guilt. I mean, I think people covered their guilt with a sense of arrogance, self-righteousness and self-justification. So this was for the people down here, you know, you heard people in the local shops saying, 'They're wild. They're different to us. They're different.'

ROBINSON.   When in reality there are more similarities than differences.

KERRIGAN.   That's the thing. When Máirtín' brought me up to the North, that was the first time I was physically and mentally North. It's also something that's really big. People are talking about it now, that a lot of people in the South, my generation, never went North of the border. Back then though the partition really became a mental as well as a psychological thing. It was certainly a physical thing.

INT. APARTMENT - NIGHT

KERRIGAN.   'It was in another lifetime'. It is 1983. It is Jack's birthday party, which he intended to be a statement, so he welcomes us in drag:

> I'd first met him in 1981 at one of the big demos. When the second hunger strike began. Máirtín and I were carrying our *Gays Against H-Block Armagh* banner for the second time in Dublin. Tarlach joined us from Derry, boosting our confidence with the sheer joy of his enthusiasm for what we were doing. The protest was large but the stewards were determined that we made a big impression. They were instructing us to spread out — three to a line — so we fitted neatly across the painted bed sheet.
>
> Jack was the steward and Tarlach knew he was gay because he'd slept with him. Tarlach told us Jack had only recently been released from Portlaoise Prison after almost nine years. Jack was a sturdy compact guy in his mid-thirties whose close-cropped hair was already thinning. He had the air of a martinet as he shouted commands. Reeking of tightly wound testosterone, strutting along the pavement, marshalling the protest. It was the first time I actually came across someone for whom the word 'ramrod' fitted perfectly.
>
> In 1983, Jack was still tightly wound on the night of his birthday. Since his return from a year in Denmark he was burning to display his changed attitude to sexuality, hence, the welcoming us in drag. Whether one judged the

INT. APARTMENT – NIGHT

drag successful or not depended on what one thought was being attempted. A hint of this was in the soundtrack of the Culture Club record that was playing as the party got started: 'Do you really want to hurt me?' With a loose hippy dress and veils swirling about, he succeeded in lightening his ramrod physique. However, the lampshade like hat and the heavily smeared on make-up made the effect comical for those of us in the Gay Collective. At least we were laughing with him. Others weren't.

I was already friendly with Brian, who had been in Portlaoise during the seventies with Jack. Máirtín and I used to go around to Brian's and his girlfriend's place on Sandymount Strand, smoking weed as we discussed politics and life. It was from Brian that I learned that Jack had stood out in prison, having had political status on an IRA wing. These rights allowed the political prisoners to organise their own schedule and wear their own clothes. Their command structure was efficient but relaxed and many chilled by smoking marijuana. Jack stood out because he had rigid self-discipline. Every morning at 6.30am he emptied the contents of his cell into the corridor, cleaning it from top to bottom and then putting everything back carefully and precisely. He spent hours daily on a gym routine which had given him the chiseled body he'd left prison with.

In September 1982 Jack told us he was taking time out — he was going to Denmark. There, comrades would help him find his feet and he could think things over. During Jack's year in Denmark, people in Dublin were getting worried about him as stories were floating back that he was behaving strangely. Living in a commune. Dressing in female attire. I assured people Jack was just pushing boundaries.

We lesbians and gay men made up over a third of the party; the rest were comrades from the Irish Republican Movement and Jack's mates. Jack's statement was primarily aimed at them and so they felt provoked, not amused. After all they had known him as a member of an IRA active service unit and some had spent years in jail together.

Oifig an Taoisigh
Office of the Taoiseach

24 August, 1982.

Mr. Charles Kerrigan,
28, Windsor Avenue,
Fairveiw,
Dublin   3.

Dear Mr. Kerrigan,

My colleague, Mr. Sean Doherty, T.D., Minister for Justice, has been in touch with me in response to representations which I have made on your behalf, regarding your arrest and detention by members of the Gardai on 1st March last.

The position is that the Garda authorities say that you were arrested at 8.20 a.m. on 1st March under Section 30 of the Offences against the State Act, 1939 in the course of Garda investigations into serious crimes.   You were detained in Rathfarnham Garda station and relaeased at 6.15 p.m. when the Gardai were satisfied that you were not involved in crimes under investigation. The Gardai say that while you were detained in custody, you were treated properly in accordance with the law and that the regulations regarding the arrest and detention of prisoners were complied with.   They deny that you were verbally abused because of your alleged sexual orientation.

If you feel that I can be of further assistance to you in the future, please do not hesitate to contact me.

With kindest regards,

Yours sincerely,

Taoiseach.

INT. APARTMENT – NIGHT

On the second of April 1982, we'd attempted to launch *Gays Against Imperialism* in the symbolically significant location of Liberty Hall. All the symbolism in the world couldn't disguise our failure to resonate with the gay and lesbian communities. We would later regroup and set up the *Dublin Lesbian & Gay Collective*. It had taken off instead.

When he returned from Denmark in spring 1983, Jack crashed in the house I shared with several others on Windsor Avenue. He was transformed: the experience of sexual freedom and acceptance in Copenhagen had liberated him. He threw himself energetically back into politics and the *Dublin Lesbian & Gay Collective*.

Jack's birthday party was his way of confronting his comrades with his sexually liberated persona. But it was also his way of confronting the *Dublin Lesbian & Gay Collective* with the reality of anti-imperialist politics. I saw all this in the middle of the dance floor. Dancing. Getting drunk.

The party was well underway by midnight and I was happily drunk and moving as best I could with the music in the crowded room. 'Two tribes went to war' — the *Frankie Goes to Hollywood's* anthem — thumped out of the speakers like a marching tune. Without any conscious directions, those who were dancing had formed four lines of about eight people each, facing each other. Our moves became aggressive to the beat. Boots and shoes hammered on the floor making the boards springy. We were moving towards and away from each other.

There was an exhilaration that grew and became ecstatic for me — Pat, who was next to me said in my ear, 'there's a strange atmosphere here, what is going on?' That's when I became conscious of the tension in the room. I saw we'd formed two units: the Republicans and the gays. We carried on dancing like this for a couple of more high energy tunes.

This moment was highly symbolic of the times. We were all very much on the fringes of society. Ireland had started out

GAYS AGAINST IMPERIALISM

LAUNCHING RALLY

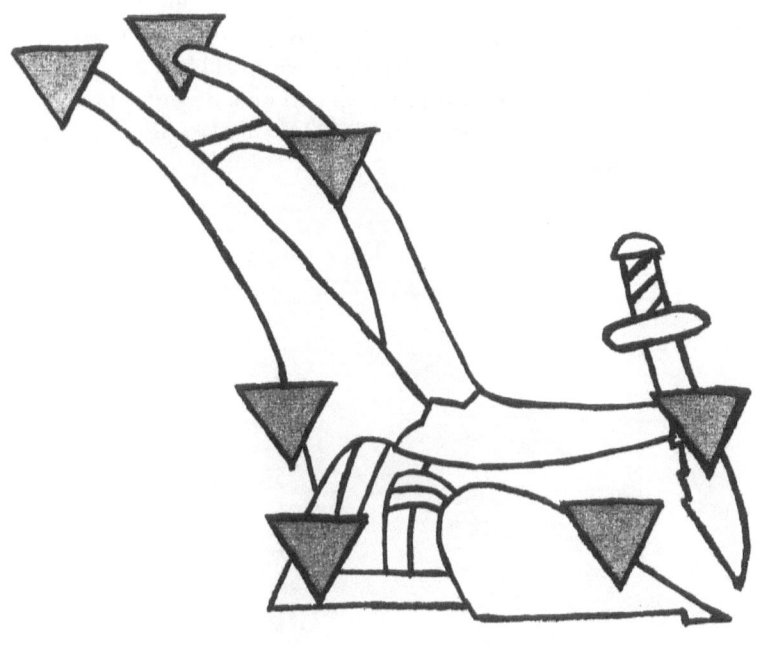

**Bernie McAliskey   Fergus O'Hare
Rita O'Hare   Tony O'Hara   Liz Noonan
Speakers from Women in Struggle & GAI**

LIBERTY HALL

8pm   2 April 1982   **50p**

INT. APARTMENT - NIGHT

on a decade of financial disasters and a growing poverty that would challenge us all to survive. We had seen ten prisoners die on the hunger strike; Sinn Féin was fighting internally. In September that year we would be scarred by the viciousness of the Abortion Referendum and would carry on into defeats on divorce and other issues for the rest of that decade. Internationally, Ronald Reagan and Maggie Thatcher would successfully undo much of the political and social progress of the previous decades since World War II. The AIDS tsunami seemed just a rip curl on a distant shore. By the end of the eighties many found themselves just clinging to driftwood.

INT. HOTEL - DAYTIME

ROBINSON.   I did notice that, all these changing names in the movement.

KERRIGAN.   So we kept changing names. The 20 or 30 of us anyway. Changing hats to suit what we needed, always with a strong ideological position. We were fighting on two fronts. We were fighting within the gay scene because people there were dismissing us as provocateurs and lunatics. Progressive, left wing people in other organisations, which were straight, supported us. But people in the gay movement would never support us.

ROBINSON.   How do you mean?

KERRIGAN.   People in the gay movement used to say things to us like, 'Well, aren't they all Catholic Nationalist, right wing people in the North. Aren't they all anti-gay, et cetera?' I would reply, 'Well, some of them are, because they've never met gay people.' We're there with our banner and I said, 'Yes, it is confrontational, but I believe that's the only way.' Again this is part of our critique which foregrounded street politics and face-to-face activism over courtroom politics.

ROBINSON.   Theory over life…

KERRIGAN.   …theory over life stuff, yes. The only way things change is by actually talking to people.

INT. HOTEL – DAYTIME

ROBINSON. Weren't there issues that transcended the borders though?

KERRIGAN. Well, that's the precise success of partition: it divided all the social as well as political movements. There was unity and agreement on the key objectives, for example in women's liberation.

ROBINSON. Like the contraception issue?

KERRIGAN. Women were bringing contraception from Northern Ireland into the Republic as a form of protest. However, the H Block Armagh Campaign divided the women's movement because the female Republican prisoners were in Armagh protesting their status. Many mainstream feminists did not see this as a feminist issue. *Gays Against Imperialism* was a parallel to the feminist movement because mainstream gay activists also didn't see the relevance of anti-partition politics to the gay issue.

ROBINSON. Why should it have relevance though?

KERRIGAN. That's what *Gays Against Imperialism* confronts. The reasons why conservative politics thrived both North and South is because imperialist power divides and conquers.

ROBINSON. Was the contraception issue close to *Gays Against Imperialism*?

KERRIGAN. Well, yes, when I met Máirtín he was a representative of the Contraceptive Action Program which united feminist, socialist and student movements to ensure contraception was made available.

ROBINSON. How?

KERRIGAN. By breaking the law in the South by selling contraceptives directly to people. In the North it was already legally available. Things like that only dramatized the imperial absurdity of partition. Contraception was available in Newry, but fifteen minutes down the road it was illegal.

Party (the 'Stickies') who are quite strong in the Trade union movement and the media - they hold important posts in R.T.E. (Radio and T.V.) and their 3 T.D.s currently hold the balance of power in the Dail (parliament). They are fervently anti-republican now despite their origins in Official I.R.A./Sinn Fein.

And now back to Liz Noonan and things:-
Liz Noonan's campaign and the I.P.P.C., which is the abortion referral service are badly in need of MONEY. Abortion and lesbianism are both unpopular causes in Ireland, so I would really like to encourage people in Britain to raise lots of money for them.

Liz needs £450, while I.P.C.C. is about £2500 in debt and is having to lay off two workers despite a great demand for their services. I.P.C.C. have no hope of getting grants from any charity or government agency in Ireland.

Another thing I'd like to mention is the harassment of gay men and women in Dublin and Cork and elsewhere. A gay man was murdered 3 weeks ago, and this gave the Garda (police) an excuse to launch a big campaign against homosexuals, pulling in loads of gays, fingerprinting, photographing and forcing them to give names and addresses of other gay men and lesbians. If people stand up for their rights, then the Garda phone up their work and homes.

The two main gay organisations in the south are not protesting, they are co-operating with the Garda. The only organisation standing out against this harassment is Gays Against Imperialism, a group in Dublin with more members in Belfast. Some women and men from G.A.I. went to Armagh for International Women's Day, and the group supports all anti-imperialist events. They called on Sinn Fein, P.D. and the I.R.S.P., etc, to back them at a picket outside Pearse St. police barracks, to protest about the attacks on gays by the Garda

Things are also very difficult for gays and lesbians in the North of Ireland, because of the Kincora Boys Home "affair". This has resulted in a hunt against all homosexuals, specially lesbians and gays who work with young people, eg. teachers, etc.

INT. HOTEL – DAYTIME   110.

ROBINSON.   Did the AIDS epidemic then also affect these campaigns for contraception?

KERRIGAN.   Yes, very much so. The whole situation changed dramatically with AIDS because condoms became central to saving gay men's lives. So as events changed, so did our practice.

ROBINSON.   And names.

KERRIGAN.   And names. The gay men involved in *Dublin Lesbian & Gay Collective* became *Gay Health Action*, because the epidemic was taking up so much energy and leaving no time for anything else.

ROBINSON.   This was in 1985?

KERRIGAN.   Yes, I was doing all this stuff for *Gay Health Action* three nights a week and the weekends too. There was so much work and workshops.

ROBINSON.   Work around AIDS prevention became the singular issue, but it wasn't solely a gay issue. How did all that play out?

KERRIGAN.   There's one instance in 1986 when *Gay Health Action* was going and we had no money. I said 'Well, look. I'm going to the commercial spaces here.' I went to the gay sauna in Dublin called The Gym, and to be fair, I went in there and I'd never been inside the sauna. I went to the counter and I said I was coming from *Gay Health Action* and that I was trying to raise funds. I met the guy called, I can't remember his name now, but he was very well known in Dublin. I explained what I wanted, and he said, 'Well, what are you looking for?' I said 'It's going to cost £150, or whatever, to produce and print this leaflet.' I said, 'I'm looking around for donations.' He said, 'Well, okay, I'll give you £50.' So he put his hand in the till and gave me £50, and that was it. No receipt or anything.

I went to another guy whose name, again, won't come to me, he wrote an autobiography. He was running another gym and a B&B with his lover and I asked for money to produce the leaflet and he just laughed in my face. He said, 'Cathal, I'm a respectable businessman. You are a loony lefty Trot. You have got *Gay Health Action* going, and if this works, you want to win credibility with the population and with other gays because you're doing this work. You want me to give you money so that you can do that, so that you can create a society which would destroy my business.'

ROBINSON. He thought the whole AIDS awareness action was actually a ploy?

KERRIGAN. No, he rightly analyzed it. We initiated *Gay Health Action*, the *Cork Gay Collective* and the *Dublin Lesbian and Gay Collective*, so it wasn't coming from *National Gay Federation*. It was coming from us on the left and we had control of it because we were open to people getting involved, but there were really only about eight of us running it from that side.

ROBINSON. I don't get it, was this guy saying that you're going to claim credit?

KERRIGAN. It was not the work we were doing which he objected to, but it was the idea that *we* were doing it.

ROBINSON. Ah, I see.

KERRIGAN. Because if it's good work, then we were going to claim credit for it, so the reformists couldn't say they did it, it wasn't done by the businesses. Now, I challenged him and said 'Look, you know well that's really disgraceful. What are you going to do?' And he said 'Well, okay, I am going to do something,' and he did, to be fair. He went out and he founded a charity to supply and help St. James's Hospital to cope with AIDS patients. Now, whether we would have ever gained respect for our left and Republican views was another issue, but what he was saying was that's how politics work. You get respect from people and then you try and say 'Well, if you respect me, I actually have these other ideas, which you might be interested in.' You know?

INT. HOTEL – DAYTIME

ROBINSON. That's the worst part of partisan politics, and that form of popular manipulation.

KERRIGAN. That's why David Norris would have been very suspicious of us as well. Quite rightly, because we totally criticized him and as I say, it was actually the activism around *Gay Health Action* that made us more visible.

ROBINSON. But wasn't AIDS something that the government had to address at some point through the Department of Health?

KERRIGAN. Yes, but the Department of Health was saying 'Well, the Department of Justice says this is an illegal activity. So we can't support any of your actions.'

ROBINSON. What? AIDS activism was illegal because homosexual sex was *technically* still illegal in the State?

KERRIGAN. Because homosexuality was illegal, yes.

ROBINSON. I would have thought with something so serious as AIDS the technicality of the law wouldn't still hold?

KERRIGAN. That's the really shocking thing. Confronted with this bureaucratic stonewalling, I was forced to change my attitude to David Norris's legal campaign.

ROBINSON. I mean, that was why I was surprised that you didn't support it before. But, well, actually, AIDS wasn't a social factor in 1981, so I suppose everything is surprising in retrospect.

KERRIGAN. Yes, the law was in fact killing gay men and our government were the agents. A government department was saying, 'You're producing a leaflet advising men how to have sex in an epidemic. That's illegal because gay sex is illegal.'

ROBINSON. So the Department of Justice wouldn't let the Department of Health do their job actually, and *Gay Health Action* did it?

KERRIGAN. Exactly, they successfully cut off funding through the

PUBLIC MEETING

The Politics of AIDS

Speakers:

Cathal O Ciarragain (Gay Health Action)
Derval Murray (World Health Organisation)

**Tuesday 4th July
7.30pm**

Kinlay House
Lord Edward Street
(next to Christ Church)

Organised by the
Irish Critical Studies Group

INT. HOTEL – DAYTIME

>
> Department of Health but we managed to get funding through our connections in the Trade Union movement. Because the economy was in crisis at the time under the government of Bertie Ahern and Charlie Haughey, who had what we called the *National Wage Agreements*. Wage controls basically. There was huge unemployment at the time so there were employment schemes set up for people on welfare. We had set up interactions and we needed people to work on AIDS awareness activism.

ROBINSON. So the activism was funded through employment schemes or something?

KERRIGAN. We actually got one of these employment schemes for *Gay Health Action*, with the support of the Trade Union movement.

ROBINSON. Trade Unions were crucial then.

KERRIGAN. Yes, we had people like Mattie Merrigan, and John, John from, from, I don't know… John Mitchell. We had broad support in the Trade Union movement.

ROBINSON. Was there a sense then, like probably the rest of the world around that time, that AIDS was a gay disease only, and therefore not an urgent public health problem?

KERRIGAN. Absolutely. What happened with the story is that we applied to the Department of Labour for two further positions. When the issue came up, they said 'They received a note from the Department of Justice saying this scheme can't go forward anymore. It's an illegal activity.'

ROBINSON. That's a messed up use of the law.

KERRIGAN. The Trade Unions just blew it out of the water though. They said 'Listen, we're not going to put up with this bullshit and nonsense, if you go on with this, we're going to walk out of here now and the whole thing is going to implode.' Next thing, the Department of Justice just dropped it. Through the papers, they said, 'sorry, okay, we'll go ahead, we'll give Gay Health Action the funding.'

ROBINSON. Such flaky bureaucracy behind life and death...

KERRIGAN. ...And we just had to get the support of Trade Unions. It was also the parallel of Ireland. You know, we talked before about consistency being an issue, of people in Ireland not being consequent. Here you had a government wherein gay sex was illegal. You had one government department refusing to fund our leaflets and you had another department funding our workers. So it was actually that inconsistency that allowed us to move forward with our work.

ROBINSON. You mean in an ironic sense?

KERRIGAN. So the irony is the lack of consequent thinking, which I criticized, turned in this instance to be beneficial. About AIDS being perceived wrongly as only a 'gay disease', it was probably the same as in Ronald Reagan's America, that it was the four H's: homosexuals, heroin addicts, hemophiliacs, and Haitians.

ROBINSON. While it was initially thought that AIDS only infected gay men, it must have spread through society quickly.

KERRIGAN. Yes, there was a huge intravenous drug problem in Dublin too. Heroin. It was really epidemic. Nothing was done to warn people and HIV spread from needle use. So we started liaising with the inner city Dublin organizations. That gave us a lot of credibility with the working class parties. They saw us working with these communities and they were really grateful because everybody else just walked away from them. We were actually trying to work with them by doing workshops, giving them what information we knew so they could go out and do what they needed to do.

Second thing is that with the hemophiliacs, on the other hand, it was discovered that there was actually a major infection in Ireland. Don't want to go too far into this, but there

INT. HOTEL – DAYTIME

> was a shortage of Factor 8, they got international supplies which were infected with HIV. Remember, there was no test back then for HIV.

ROBINSON. What happened next?

KERRIGAN. What happened is we made contact with the head of the Hemophilia Society, but they didn't want to touch us. They spent all the time keeping a distance from us. Their policy was, 'we as hemophiliacs are not like these other people. We're not like these drug users, or homosexuals. We hemophiliacs are a very limited population and we can get concessions from the government.' They also had legal support, because there was a legal contract when they were getting the blood from the *Irish Blood Transfusion Service*. We made those links and we consciously tried to broaden that because with *Gay Health Action*, it was a conscious thing to use the word gay in the title. Like *Gays Against Imperialism*.

ROBINSON. You mean in relation to the epidemic?

KERRIGAN. If this is affecting gay men, if we don't use the word gay, gay men will be forgotten about. But then a year in we decided we're going to have problems as *Gay Health Action* getting resources.

> So we decided the strategy was to broaden it out by forming *AIDS Action Alliance* and get the inner city communities involved, get women involved, and try and get the hemophiliacs involved. We formed it and we did get people involved. What happened of course, within a couple of years, is that it took off and got a life of its own and *Gay Health Action* was partially sidelined. We set it up as a front organization. We saw it as a way that the government would talk to us too, but of course it took on a life of its own. Very rapidly we were in a minority and were kind of pushed aside. I don't know if that answers your question.

EXT. RAISED GARDEN - MORNING

ROBINSON.   Mario Mieli's book *Homosexuality and Liberation: Towards a Gay Critique*, foregrounded a concern regarding the splitting of Gay and Women's rights. Mieli's position was that, in some ways, the patriarchal capitalist economy could change only by uniting multiple causes, through dismantling the sexism even within the Left. Were you aware of Mieli's *Toward a Gay Communism* — it seems to feed into *Gays Against Imperialism: For Gay Liberation through National Liberation?*

KERRIGAN.   Oh yeah, absolutely. I read Mario Mieli's book. I found it hard going to be honest. It's very theoretical and very ahead of its time, pre-empting trans identity and gender neutrality. That was a very difficult, invisible thing back in 1980, when I got the book and read it. It's this heavy Italian Marxist theory and I was trying to plow through it but I'm not a theoretician. The second thing was that I was shocked by how far out Mieli was. I was very inspired but nobody else seemed to be. I would give the book to people to read and they would say, 'God, I can't read that. I tried reading that and I couldn't get past page five'. When Mieli committed suicide in 1983, for me it was a major personal blow. I don't know the details around it, do you?

ROBINSON.   It is a difficult book, but the concepts around the connections of gay men and women were probably not that easy to articulate in academia. He committed suicide just before the publishing of his first novel, for what seems to be fear over its reception. It was published just after his death, but

EXT. RAISED GARDEN - MORNING

                  the Mieli family, who seemed to be very wealthy, had all the copies destroyed. In 1994 the book was re-published, from what I can gather from a photocopy of a pirated manuscript. I have a copy of the 1994 edition, but don't read Italian, so I can't read it properly, but I would love to. Not because of its tragic publishing history at all, but because it is literature from someone who tried a new way to experiment with political imagination.

KERRIGAN. In a very dark way, I felt I could understand why Mieli did it with Reagan and Thatcher going crazy. The world was going backwards so fast and we felt we were losing everything. I just remember feeling so affected by that suicide, it was such a declaration that our revolution isn't going to happen. We're not going to change the world after all and that feeling of wanting to get out because it's not worth going on.

ROBINSON. Like a sign of defeat or something?

KERRIGAN. To me, yes, at least that was my interpretation. There is a huge amount of loss and uncertainty, like any suicide of a political activist. International solidarity and communication is very important.

ROBINSON. I found the letters between you and activist Simon Nkoli very moving, and the connection between South Africa and the Irish question a very particular intervention in the birds eye view of the *Irish Queer Archive*. I also began to interpret the photocopy in a different way then, when in the letters Nkoli mentions that he wants you to send him an IRA t-shirt? I have to admit, I was taken aback by that…

KERRIGAN. …I can understand that.

ROBINSON. But then as I progressed through the letters the IRA connection seemed almost peripheral.

KERRIGAN. The letter correspondence between Simon and myself lasted over three or four years, and actually, I am just making conversation with him. I remember thinking at the time: what

EXT. RAISED GARDEN – MORNING

                should I tell this guy who is in prison in South Africa? So I tell him about Ireland. And this famous t-shirt he wanted? I can't remember what the t-shirt was now, but they would have produced t-shirt's supporting the IRA, with Bobby Sands, or with a ballot in one hand and a gun in the other.

ROBINSON. In one later letter he tells you he receives the t-shirt and he wears it in prison.

KERRIGAN. Yes, but fellow prisoners tell him to take it off as it is too confrontational, it would cause more trouble for him with the negotiations that were going on.

ROBINSON. You were part of the group organising the *Gays Against Apartheid* event, but how did you start the letter correspondence with Simon in the first place?

KERRIGAN. It was through the *International Lesbian and Gay Association* that I started to write to Simon. The people who were involved there contacted the international gay movement to make people aware of Simon Nkoli, a gay man involved in the anti-apartheid struggle. It was publicized in the *ILGA Bulletin* and one of the things that we welcomed in this was that there was a gay aspect to the struggle. So for instance we were all supportive of the anti-apartheid struggle, but that was run by heterosexuals, so the whole tone was 'well, what has anti-apartheid got to do with gay rights, of course we support it but it has nothing got to do with it'. So this was a link for us as here you have a gay, anti-apartheid activist who is in prison and who needed support. So it was two-fold, recognizing sexuality as part of a struggle, not distinct from it.

Simon Nkoli was in the African National Congress (ANC), and it was getting very fierce in the mid 1980s. The ANC was building up links in the communities and building protests in the townships. The South African regime wanted to quash these protests so it started to use the law by making the ANC illegal and stating that these people were involved in terrorism. Sine Féin and the Republicans were very supportive of the ANC. In West Belfast, one of the murals

EXT. RAISED GARDEN – MORNING

supported the ANC and the anti-apartheid struggle. From the point of view of the IRA armed struggle, the ANC had a similarly armed wing, which was admittedly very weak and didn't get a lot of media publicity. In the end the ANC down played the armed struggle, but it did exist.

ILGA publicised Simon Nkoli in the gay movement. We didn't see this as exploitive though, it was simply the nexus of the two aspects of anti-apartheid and the gay struggle overlapping. ILGA were calling for solidarity in the form of a letter writing campaign. It didn't start as a detailed correspondence. It started out as a postcard of solidarity. I don't know what the image was as I didn't keep a record. So the first letter in the IQA is his reply. Presumably he had received a lot of correspondence from around the world. So that is where the letters begin.

ROBINSON. I wondered how Nkoli might have viewed Ireland, and the situation in the North?

KERRIGAN. Well, the perception of the IRA in South Africa and many other places around the world was as a National Liberation Struggle, so that was the same in El Salvador and Nicaragua for example. So you had people in Ireland, who were not Nationalists or Republicans, but were Liberal, Social Democrats and Labour who supported Anti-Apartheid, who supported the El Salvador struggle, Nicaragua's struggle, and they would be embarrassed by these people saying, 'but you have a Liberation Army who struggle against British Imperialism.' The mainstream political parties found they had a theoretical dilemma and difficulty here. If you look at this internationally and step back from the closeness to Ireland, the IRA are not terrorists, they are fighting against an Imperialist power and this is the history of colonialism and the unfinished business of the 1920s. So that is what Simon Nkoli was referring to, but I could understand why the t-shirt would seem shocking to you.

ROBINSON. As I say that shock was only peripheral, there seemed to have been a friendship formed throughout the letters.

KERRIGAN.   So that is how it all began with the letter exchanges, and as you can see over time in the letters I put in my own personal life. The breaking up of a relationship, going in and out of contracts for work, going off to Greece on holidays, so you get all this personal stuff, because that is what you fill the letters with. Simon was lucky in that the case against him collapsed, and then he was supporting the others who were imprisoned. In 1988, ILGA were still in touch with him and they were funnelling funds and support. The South African gay organisation did not support Simon, because it was predominantly white. Simon challenged them on this and they came under huge pressure internationally as the South African gay organization wanted to be seen as liberal, when in fact they were racist. All these contradictions came on board, when the South African Gay Rights movement said, 'well we are just fighting for gay rights, and we are not going to bother about that fact we are living in an apartheid society, where black people are denied their rights.' So Simon was arguing that with them and much later he made a kind of peace with them.

Simon set up a separate organization focused on the townships. So with all the complications of the struggle, and the personal and the political side of it, it was never easy for him.

ROBINSON.   Did you ever meet with Simon?

KERRIGAN.   Yes, in 1988 he got support from Sweden, they sponsored him to come to the ILGA conference in Vienna, and coincidentally Kieran Rose and I funded ourselves to go and lobby at this five day conference. It was very powerful, we met with Dennis Altman there too. We party and there are huge fights at it because there are conflicting agendas in the international Gay Rights movement. One of the things was that people in South America were saying, 'please do not send envelopes addressed to the homosexual movement' because we are under attack, receiving death threats and people have been killed for being identified as gay. So in many ways it was also a fight against ignorance, that one local gay rights situation was not the same as another and so on.

EXT. RAISED GARDEN – MORNING

ROBINSON. The dangers of universality...

KERRIGAN. ...the universality of *Liberation* is a great aspiration, but it's trying to unite people across very different cultures and situations. Simon was also there and we got on very well with him. He was going to come to Ireland, but didn't make it in the end.

ROBINSON. Did you ever meet in person again?

KERRIGAN. I lived in Amsterdam from 1992 to 1999 and kept in touch, but those letters aren't deposited in the *Irish Queer Archive*. The last time I saw him was in 1998 when the Gay Games were held in Amsterdam and Simon got in touch to say he was attending. I took Simon to this bar, called Route 66 on Kirk Straat. I had had a brief affair with one of the people who ran the bar. Simon and I sat at the bar as it was fairly early for Amsterdam, but the thing about this bar was that it was frequented by a lot of Americans. Particularly gay CIA Agents going back and forth to the Middle East. They liked to party in Amsterdam and this was the bar they liked to go to. Once I took a Bulgarian friend from work there, and he insisted on leaving because the place was full of American spies and he was a former Communist...

ROBINSON. ...Wait, let's not get *Tinker, Tailor, Soldier, Spy* here.

KERRIGAN. Hahahaha

ROBINSON. What did Simon think of the bar?

KERRIGAN. Simon and I were sitting at the bar and we were just going to have one drink because he was tired and he had to get up the next morning for a workshop. We had a drink and then this guy rings the bell. He was told by the barman that in the Netherlands that if you ring the bell you have to buy everyone in the bar a round of drinks. So the guy rang the bell again and he was buying everyone a drink. So as the guy was buying we decided to have a brandy instead of beer. The guy rang the bell again so we had another. We were fairly drunk by the time we were leaving.

The conversation at the bar though was very sad. Simon had full-blown AIDS at that stage. He didn't look sick, but it was very difficult for him at the time. He would die six months later. I was being myself so we argued about politics. I remembered I expressed an opinion, and Simon said I didn't understand the South African context. We didn't argue or anything, but just disagreed. We got talking more and Simon told me that he was still suffering from the torture he suffered in prison, waking up with night sweats. This really shocked and upset me, and after the bar, I walked him up the road. We embraced and that was the last I heard or saw from him. At the end of 1998 I saw the newspaper piece that he had died.

ROBINSON. Heart-breaking. After reading the letters in the archive, I saw a documentary by Bev Ditsie and Nicky Newman called *Simon and I*.[49] Ditsie, who is a singer and civil rights activist, was the first 'out' lesbian to address a United Nations Conference, saying that lesbian rights were women's rights. The whole documentary is about Ditsie's close friendship and adoration of Simon. The film is like a love song that goes through the complexity, joy and pain of personal relationships that run parallel to public, political ones. For me, what was so striking about *Simon and I* is that it really goes through the pain of loss, change and no change in the political landscape. It shows the violence afflicted upon lesbians after the AIDS epidemic hit, and in some ways even their abandonment by gay men. At one point in the documentary Ditsie tells how her focusing on feminist activism put her in a position where she had to break with the gay rights' movement. This seems to be a reoccurring narrative throughout late 20th Century Gay History.

---

49. Simon & I, A film by Bev Ditsie and Nicky Newman, South Africa, 2002, 52 minutes http://www.wmm.com/filmcatalog/pages/c606.shtml (last accessed 09.09.16)

EXT. RAISED GARDEN – MORNING

KERRIGAN. Absolutely. I haven't seen the documentary; I think I would find it upsetting.

ROBINSON. The film doesn't try to hide complexity, nor is it angry, it is upsetting in parts, but it also tells a very important story. It is the *queer friendship* that endures.

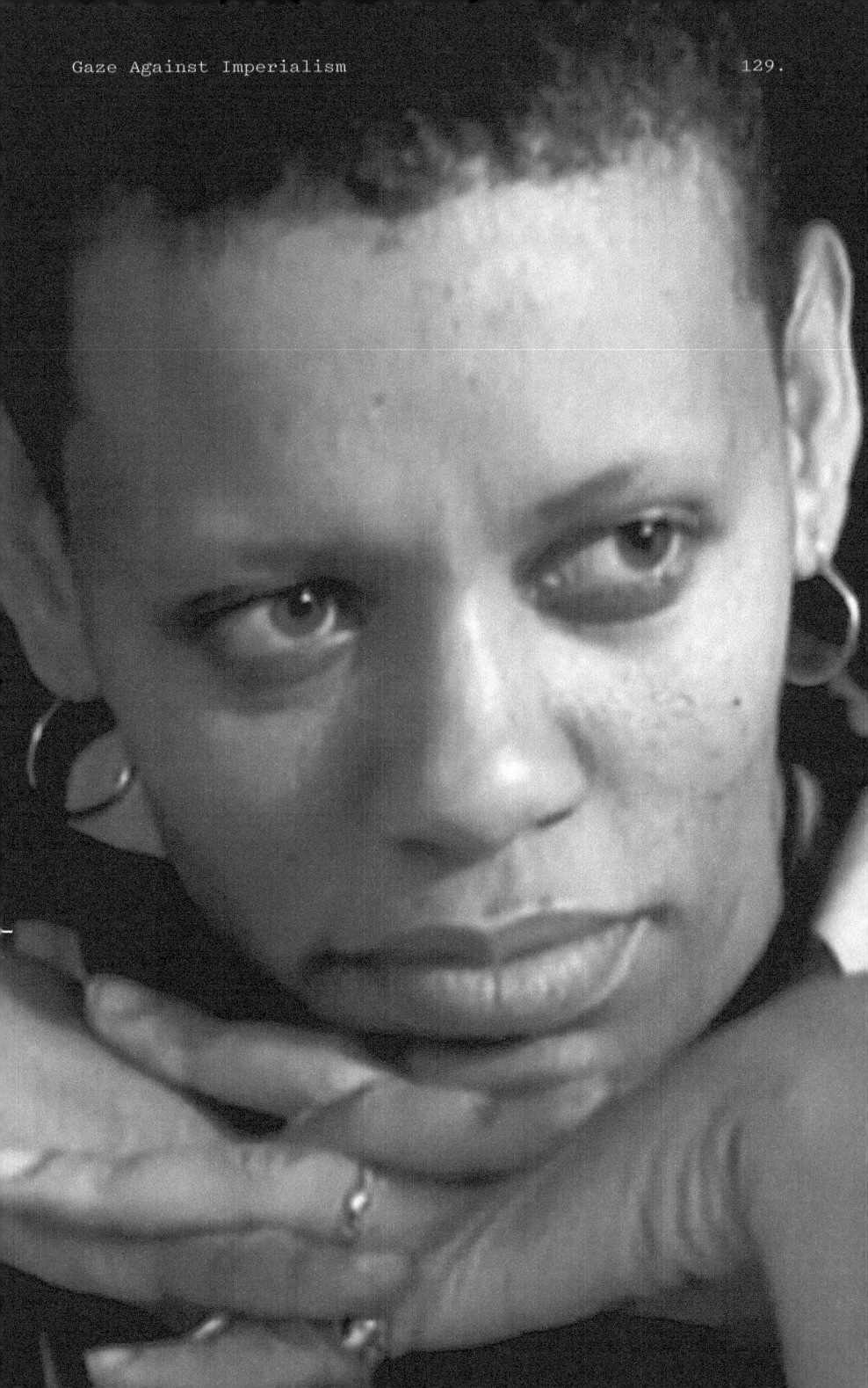

INT. TERRACED HOUSE - EVENING

ROBINSON. I was reminded of a small story you wrote in one of the earlier draft transcripts, and what we were saying before about changing names. The story touched on how the meanings of phrases become something else, and even change entirely, in the moments and years after a protest.

KERRIGAN. What was the story?

ROBINSON. It was about two friends of yours who were at a protest and they had a banner reading 'Queers Against Pinkwashing'. Teenagers shouted at these friends of yours after the protest, because they thought that 'Queer' was meant as an insult?

KERRIGAN. Young teens, yes. So what happened is that Sue and Martin, who are long-time activists in their 60s, were at a protest to support Palestine, in the centre of Dublin. There was another friend of theirs, Omar, with them at this protest, and it was actually he who was carrying a placard that read 'Queers Against Pinkwashing'. Only people who were at the protest would know that the detailed background of 'Queers Against Pinkwashing' is that the Israeli government keeps saying they are the only true democracy in the Middle East because it has European human rights values. The example the government gives is 'look at homosexuals in our society, they have gay rights'. The message is of a tolerant, open, Western society respecting human rights.

ROBINSON. Well, the whole concept of Pinkwashing is very complex.

INT. TERRACED HOUSE – EVENING

KERRIGAN. Yes, but the argument of course, from the point of view of supporting Palestinians, is that they are blind to what they are doing to the Palestinian and the Arab-Israeli population. Omar, because he comes from the Middle East, wanted to raise these questions with the 'Queers Against Pinkwashing' banner.

ROBINSON. Ah, so it was not Sue and Martin's placard?

KERRIGAN. He gave it to them to bring home as he was going out with friends. Now, the reason I mentioned the story is because this anecdote is shorthand for a very big concept.

ROBINSON. Huge.

KERRIGAN. How you understand things is about being engaged in certain circles.

ROBINSON. Ways of speaking and listening, even misunderstanding. Education, class, all come into play, something blasphemous in one accent might seem critical in another etc.[50]

KERRIGAN. Absolutely, even to realise what this 'Queers Against Pinkwashing' placard actually meant, you'd have to be in certain circles.

ROBINSON. But how did the teenagers see the placard? Were they at the protest?

KERRIGAN. No, this was after the protest.

---

50. See Talal Assad: 'The tendency to emphasize manner of expression – to see blasphemy in terms of form rather than content – had, however, some interesting legal implications: vulgar working class speech was less protected than the polite speech of the middle and upper classes. A scholar who has studied blasphemy trials in nineteenth-century England calls them "class crimes of language" on account of the class bias they indicate.' Is Critique Secular: Blasphemy, Injury, and Free Speech, New York: Fordham University Press, 2013, p 29

ROBINSON. Ah, I see.

KERRIGAN. Sue and Martin were carrying the placard home with them. And so there they were, two people, a man and woman in their 60s, looking laid back after a protest. They're strolling back at about half past five through this district in central Dublin. These teenagers then see these two elderly people and they're carrying this placard. They see the word 'queers' 'against pinkwashing'. And 'pinkwashing', what's that? They just see 'queers against' — two negative words to them obviously — and then they just sort of start following Martin and Sue, passing them out, saying, 'Hey mister. Hey misses. What do you have against gay people?' Sue and Martin have to stop and explain that the 'against' is actually 'queer people, or gay people, against something'. Then they have to explain that the word 'queer' is actually what very progressive LGBT+ people like to call themselves now.

ROBINSON. Isn't it amazing that in 2017 there is a much bigger difference in the awareness of how different words resonate in different times? These young kids grew up seeing the successful Irish marriage referendum, yet they actually still read 'queer' as an insult that they fight against, which *is*, weirdly great, isn't it?

KERRIGAN. Yes, but it's actually a reflection of the decay of gay politics if you wish again to make parallels.

ROBINSON. Don't get me wrong, I don't think it is ironic, but maybe this story brings up things to do with...

KERRIGAN. ...but you see it is ironic, isn't it? But the irony is actually a positive irony. If they don't get the resonance of 'Queer' on the placard, the visibility of the word needs to be raised with the complexity of the struggle that gave it new political meaning. But there are other questions.

EXT. BUSY STREET - DAYTIME

ROBINSON. But I suppose everything, even community and communication, is corporatized, and privatised, now? Even the so-called 'down time' of the cognitive worker is spent using social media technology. Supplying information for its mining so as to presumably make us better consumers. But this form of 'free time' almost implies that we are not creative participants in a community where our labour has value, or power, and who knows what else? Fulfilment?

KERRIGAN. Did you go to Dublin Pride in 2017?

ROBINSON. I think the last time I was there was in 2014.

KERRIGAN. The Pride March in 2017 had so many corporate and institutional delegations, which is a debatable sign of the success of the gay rights movement as it is represented in the Irish Queer Archive. But it also featured a section in the parade and they called themselves *Working Class Queerios*. It was a disparate grouping that displayed its criticism of the mainstream movement with a sense of humour. They had a placard with the LGBT acronym that spelled out as 'LinkdIn Google Bluetooth Twitter'.

ROBINSON. Hahahah, that's great!

KERRIGAN. It included several political groupings — *People Before Profit*, *Sinn Féin*, *Labour Party*. The *Working Class Queerios* grouping were, guess what?

EXT. BUSY STREET - DAYTIME

ROBINSON. What?

KERRIGAN. Placed last in the parade. However, I read this as a sign of potential good news — with a gathering of like-minded dissenters.

ROBINSON. A case of back to the future?

KERRIGAN. It reminded me of *Gays Against Imperialism,* yes, yet all this social media technology is presenting us with more and more egos based on the number of your followers. Unlike *Gays Against Imperialism.*

ROBINSON. So politics gets drowned out by moral narcissism more than it ever has. My friend Karen mentioned a term to me... hmmmm... I forgot it now?... We were talking about when we were both in college, and in that whole period it became no longer a question of whether you used Facebook, or Bebo, or whatever was on the go then. It was just a given, nobody questioned it, rather people questioned if you didn't use social media — 'Virtue signalling!' — That's the term I was trying to remember. But over the years it was almost suspicious not to participate with social technologies that are mostly about *spending.*

KERRIGAN. Yes, and this has political consequences.

ROBINSON. It has significantly altered the whole political structure as a result of it. Not having a social media profile came to mean a kind of self-isolation.

KERRIGAN. That's the big challenge now, if you talk about the feeling of being overwhelmed by these social media influences.

ROBINSON. Social media by proxy overwhelms society whether you participate or not though. I never really expressed myself on public media platforms. That's not a judgement on them though, it is amazing how these media are used for voicing things that otherwise wouldn't be heard. I am not a luddite, but it is the 'Start Uppy' people who have zero knowledge of

KERRIGAN. social ethics but lots of information for filling holes in the marketplace that freak me out.

KERRIGAN. Like the yuppies in the 1980s?

ROBINSON. Kind of, but the new rhetoric around team building and digital products is also about playing on people's prejudice in echo chambers, pointless spending and progress.

KERRIGAN. Literally, only last week, I bought a smartphone and now I'm talking to Google.

ROBINSON. Does it beat talking to yourself?

KERRIGAN. Hahaha, you know some people might say that is a very psychoanalytic question.

ROBINSON. Hahaha, well, I should come clean: I am wary of psychoanalysis and its *creation* of symptoms.

KERRIGAN. Oh, why so?

ROBINSON. Long story.

KERRIGAN. The short version?

ROBINSON. Probably because I read *Anti-Oedipus* in 2006 and I'm trying to crawl out of it since[51]. I ordered the book after I read

---

51. Deleuze and Guattari, *Anti-Oedipus*, Continuum Impacts, 2004, p 94 and 95: 'Whence the role of names, with a magic all their own: there is no ego that identifies with races, peoples, and persons in a theater of representation, but proper names that identify races, peoples, and persons with regions, thresholds, or effects in a production of intensive quantities. The theory of proper names should not be conceived of in terms of representation; it refers instead to the class of "effects": effects that are not a mere dependence on causes, but the occupation of a domain, and the operation of a system of signs.'

EXT. BUSY STREET – DAYTIME

STOP VIOLENCE AGAINST GAYS
Protest March
Saturday 19 March 2.30pm
Liberty Hall - Fairview Park

Justice Gannon's decision in this case has shocked the country. To protest at the decision and at its implications, the Dublin Gay Collective is calling on everyone who cares for civil rights to join in a public demonstration on saturday March 19th.

Since the judgement, much has been said about the leniency of the sentences and many have called for the judges' resignation. Little, however, has been said about the hypocracy that underlies the decision. The only reason for Justice Gannon's leniency is, that despite his denials, he <u>did</u> accept the "excuse" that the gang were in the park to clear it of homosexuals. This gang has admitted more than twenty cases of planned assault and robbery, choosing as its victims gays or people who they <u>thought</u> might be gay. This premeditation should make the crime more serious, not less.

It seems instead that gays can now be beaten or killed almost with impunity. The judgement is a gross violation of our rights, and emphasises the urgent need for law reform. Because all gay male activity is illegal, the thugs in this case felt justified in beating and eventually killing people they thought of as "queers". Their activities were known to the police; detailed complaints had been made but nothing was done. This again was sexual prejudice, this time by the Gardai. It took a young man's death to spur them to action.

Suspended sentences would be a welcome and overdue reform in our legal system where pointless and damaging prison sentences are so often given. However, when almost the only step in this direction is taken in a murder case where the criminals excuse is "queer-bashing", then that is a travesty of reform. There are other cases where prejudices are equally shocking. Some years ago a judge allowed as a "mitigating" factor the excuse that the murdered victim was only a prostitute; in many rape cases an excuse is accepted that the woman contributed to the crime by not protesting enough or by being in a dark street by herself. There must be legal reform: these miserable prejudices must not form part of it.

WE DEMAND: The immediate repeal of all legislation that defines us as criminals.
The support of all political groups with concern for human rights
The participation in this important march of gays and non-gays alike.

Meet at Liberty Hall at 2.30pm. At Fairview Park a rally will be held to be addressed by Speakers from the Dublin Gay Collective and the N.G.F. (Be There)

this research report about the 'Sexual Deviance' of children displaying queer traits. The report heavily foregrounded psychoanalytic theory to support forms of reversion therapy; come to think of it, so did the targeted advertising campaigns in the early 20th Century.

KERRIGAN. Yes, like the micro targeting in social media around the Brexit and Trump campaigns. What was it about the report that angered you?

ROBINSON. The part I remember being really annoyed about in this research report was how the little boys analysed tended to rarely identify with the Princess archetype, but rather with middle-aged women characters such as the *Wicked Witch of the West*. It was such imperialising, patriarchal thinking — all about roles — with a whole sub category of attack on the femme by foregrounding the essentialism of youth and proper femininity.

KERRIGAN. Sounds like it had a personal resonance?

ROBINSON. I was in fact fascinated by the *Wicked Witch of the West* as a child, to the point that when my sister had grown out of her red shoes, I was adamant to inherit what I referred to from then on as *my good shoes*.

KERRIGAN. Hahaha .

ROBINSON. Hahahaha, they were *good*. So I suppose the report embarrassed me somehow. Here was an imaginative development wrongly framed yet still gazed upon in retrospect as a potential subject of research. So it made me very aware of researcher prejudice, projecting the symptom onto the subject, so I kind of fell upon an 'I OBJECT'!

KERRIGAN. Hahahahah. I laugh because it's just so surreal. You just can't make this up. Once there was this guy called Gabriel who I met. A Vietnamese-French Trotskyist who had loads of money and was living in Cork. So I meet him and he was fascinated by me. It turned out that he was a psychoanalyst

EXT. BUSY STREET – DAYTIME

and also a Trotskyist. First, I think I thought 'what the hell is going on here', but then I found he was totally legit. Gabriel told me his father was a Vietnamese diplomat and his mother was a French aristocrat, so he obviously came from money and was doing work for the international movement. So anyway, I end up doing psychoanalysis with him. Which is crazy.

ROBINSON. Woah, when was this?

KERRIGAN. Around 1980, the year I became the Student Union President. So I'm living at home and I am doing this therapy. It turns out for me to be very productive. It breaks up a year later with that classic fight. I suddenly discover that he is Freudian, with me going 'what the fuck?' when he said 'you need to release the heterosexual in you'.

ROBINSON. Hahahaha, there was only ever one sexuality for Freud.

KERRIGAN. And I was going 'who the fuck cares if I am half heterosexual or 2% heterosexual'. I was fighting to get a healthy homosexual in there.

ROBINSON. It must have been a really interesting process though?

KERRIGAN. It was productive, and I was only into this a while, not a lifetime. It must have been spring 1980 because I was living at home and Gabriel was challenging me about my relationship with my late father. Gabriel challenged my whole homoerotic fixation with my father as the first man I fancied, so he was confronting me with this Freudian stuff.

ROBINSON. OK, so let's avoid being Freudian, but may I be very direct about the material in the archive?

KERRIGAN. Absolutely.

ROBINSON. When we had the phone call a few years ago, we discussed how *Gays Against Imperialism* opposed the *National Gay Federation*'s legal campaign for law reform. David Norris was a crucial player, yes, but there were other legal intellects at play, like Mary Robinson, before she became President of Ireland in 1990.

KERRIGAN. Yes.

ROBINSON. At points you changed your political views quite dramatically?

KERRIGAN. Yes! Some people would see this as a sign of weakness, but I see that flexibility as vital when engaging with a continuously changing reality.

ROBINSON. Norris wrongly accused you of being involved with Provos, how do you feel about that now?

KERRIGAN. Yes, but in the 1970s I viewed the Provo's as 'individual terrorism': a Trotskyist term meaning violent actions taken by groups separate from the organised proletariat. For instance, the Red Army Faction (RAF) in Germany. In the early 1980s I changed my perspective based on my lived experience of the H-Block Armagh campaign, my visits to Belfast and Derry, and my discussions with friends.

ROBINSON. And lovers.

KERRIGAN. And lovers. In 1984 I joined Sinn Féin.

ROBINSON. And you left a year later, to focus on AIDS activism?

KERRIGAN. Yes and now, the twenty years after the *Good Friday Agreement* led to a power-sharing arrangement between Sinn Féin and the Democratic Unionist Party (DUP). People now argue that the 'armed struggle' was unnecessary. That if the peaceful mass protest movement had not been interrupted by the actions of a group in a secret army, then all that has been now achieved could have been won without the loss of thousands of lives. I feel this argument has legitimacy and I find my attempts today to justify my position back then, to be blunt: unconvincing.

EXT. BUSY STREET – DAYTIME

ROBINSON. When I brought up the material in the *Irish Queer Archive* by saying let's not be Freudian, I meant that my question was not meant to confront you with an archive of political mistake.

KERRIGAN. Well that is exactly how I experienced it reading some of the documents from 30 years that I had written but forgotten about.

ROBINSON. Does it always have to be about success?

KERRIGAN. Don't get me wrong; I think it's very important that the material is in the archive, as we all have a tendency to fictionalize our past. The archive confronts us with the full reality of what we said and did.

ROBINSON. The public scope of archives is a way to come face to face with contradictions and antagonisms that might need to be faced. It depends on how it is read...

KERRIGAN. ...and who is reading it. Absolutely.

ROBINSON. Hannah Arendt's first husband, Günther Anders – who never forgave Martin Heidegger by the way – said something like, the only way to challenge the Nihilism of techno-social life is to turn to history. I am paraphrasing, I hope correctly, but he also said we produce more than we can visualise or understand. So I felt like I was trespassing in the Irish Queer Archive at times, gazing at this material from the past that was vulnerable to be 're-read' as something it wasn't.

KERRIGAN. Yes, yes, and that is lived political reality. I have to accept that I personally made the wrong choice in supporting the armed struggle, and I don't think it is useful to play 'truth or dare' games with political struggle. My move from seeing the IRA's armed struggle as individual terrorism to then regarding it as part of a national liberation struggle was not made flippantly though. It arose from a complex situation, and a difficult period of thinking by actually going North.

ROBINSON. The 'Irish Problem' is coming back now differently with Brexit and a whole other set of questions, and fictions, so the symptom merely gets renamed.

KERRIGAN. That's imperialism[52].

ROBINSON. It's also the desire for conquest, for property, for ownership, for political personality, and that that is considered the *only* history we have to stand on is just not enough. I mean it is absurd that the British Empire was built on lands that were raped and pillaged, and what we end up with in 2016 is an imagination where a petty, *Tory* referendum has essentially voted for 'Fortress Britain'? There are serious historical amnesias going on at the moment.

KERRIGAN. And it's not just individuals who fictionalize their own past, but now whole nations are presenting new histories through right wing movements. That fictionalization involves a false image of the past that is based on conservative conformity. On our first phone call about *Gays Against Imperialism* I said one of our perceptions back then was that despite legal advances in human rights, the economic rights have not progressed to the same transformative extent.

ROBINSON. Parliamentary processes always slow things down structurally, stalling enough time for forgetting sometimes.

KERRIGAN. Absolutely.

---

52. See John A. Hobson, *Imperialism: A Study*, Edinburgh: Ballantyne, Hanson & Co, 1902, p 12: 'Though the conduct of nations in dealing with one another has commonly been determined at all times by selfish and short-sighted considerations, the conscious, deliberate adoption of this standard, at an age when the intercourse of nations and their interdependence for all essentials of human life grow ever closer, is a retrograde step fraught with grave perils to the cause of civilisation'.

EXT. BUSY STREET – DAYTIME

ROBINSON. What is perhaps a parallel to the early 1980s is that a whole new generation has seen the economic rights fought for by earlier generations being eroded nearly every day. They see, or don't see as the case may be, the public or social legislations won by your generation slowly eroded into a new form of conformity. The fury about the widespread abuse and hypocrisy being exposed means that people are fighting back through acts of direct action, but the parliamentary processes are not keeping up with the street anger.

KERRIGAN. Well, the population votes for the politicians, but maybe I misunderstood, what do you mean?

ROBINSON. Militant campaigns of the past might seem attractive on *both* sides of the left and right divide. Looking to the future, the new-borns of today are going to grow up to a very critical class conflict if climate change isn't addressed. It seems so complicated to get anything done, or say anything meaningful here and now though. Imperialism can be dismantled through widespread conscientious objections that cut through the managerial consensus. It is no longer the age of just killing the Tsar any more, is it?

KERRIGAN. No… it's not… last year I read Jonathan Lerner's *Swords in the Hands of Children: Reflections of an American Revolutionary*. He was a member of Students for a Democratic Society [SDS], which was a very successful, and peaceful direct action movement in the late 1960s. Campaigning across campuses and towns against the Vietnam War, but also for progressive causes. He describes how he sees in retrospect the tragic error made when the SDS leadership decided to go underground and become a covert violent terror group, the Weathermen. I feel it's essential to learn from the mistakes of past struggles — especially for those galvanizing in current progressive movements. But we need to be very clear that there is a difference between direct action and individual terrorism. Individual terrorism is violence carried out by a self-selected, covert group; direct action is a dramatization, or, an agitprop that may also be carried out by a self-selected group but is in the end aimed at galvanizing mass action.

Recently I've been thinking about how we in the 1980s tried to be internationalist, sending letters to Jamaica, to Simon Nkoli, the foundation of ILGA. Back then it was difficult — but today it is social media that is facilitating international contact. This should lead to a more integrated struggle and a solidarity that is deeper and more real-time.

ROBINSON. The question then is why hasn't all that social technology reflected positively back on society in terms of people having 'free time' with no market to fill?

KERRIGAN. So I suggest the challenge for today's activists then is to radically question what is wrong with the way we are organizing and representing — why the Left is not effectively using the possibilities of today's technology to create a more real meaningful solidarity that isn't just about voicing discontent. That's the thing about vision though. You have to have a vision, a policy. You know, it isn't about saying let's go back to the middle ages, back to the land, and have no modern technology.

ROBINSON. The problem is with parliamentary processes too though, but I know what you mean.

KERRIGAN. A reforming of production wouldn't necessarily have to imply taking any of the positive effects of technology away, because technology is just an instrument or tool that can make life easier and better. If we take back agency and ask for what ends do we want to use these devices, that's different. Because it is the vision of the end that determines how we use the means. How can it be done? What is the program?

ROBINSON. Hmmmmmm… when we are so entrenched in social technology, it's hard to express what we actually *need* it for now. Capitalism was always about confusing need and want, and fuck is it sublime in doing it!

KERRIGAN. Well, it is an economic war.

EXT. BUSY STREET - DAYTIME

ROBINSON. Which is a slow death. Do you know that part in the *Quare Fellow?*

KERRIGAN. No?

ROBINSON. One character said something like he found it hard to walk because of damage done to his leg because of the war. Another character asks 'which war? The economic war?'

KERRIGAN. Hahaha, but where to start?

ROBINSON. A start has to be dismantling the system of profit gains solely for neo-colonial countries that literally and figuratively offload their problems onto far away lands, and then recede, when the world they made suddenly hits home.

KERRIGAN. But this is what progressives need to present now: a vision of a better society — with concrete details and stepping-stones from the here and now and how to get there. I fear it is because the alt-right is good at this that it is succeeding.

ROBINSON. Well, the alt-right is also giving voice to diverse, petty and dangerous demands. Using basic, false narratives and symbols. There is a lack of thinking going on that starts from the erosion of education and the lack of *responsive* curriculum. A *responsive* curriculum though needs to be combined with a *responsive* parliament where the Left no longer has to revel on the marginality of itself, but rather has space to articulate new demands on how people *behave* with power.

KERRIGAN. For the left, we have only just experienced the collapse of Social Democracy in the last couple of years. Social Democracy came into power in the 1950s and 1960s, when capitalism boomed giving huge increases in profits, so that the ruling class could well afford to give concessions to workers. But in 2008, capitalism almost collapsed, and the fact that it didn't is amazing to me. Then, the profit surplus to feed Social Democracy evaporated, and we've had austerity for the last decade, which is why, in my view, Social Democracy has collapsed.

ROBINSON.   It lost a material basis?

KERRIGAN.   Yes, and on top of that the leaderships of Social Democracy had become assimilated into these power structures and became the implements of austerity in many countries.

ROBINSON.   Your analysis shares points of departure with political theorist Chantal Mouffe[53].

KERRIGAN.   How so?

ROBINSON.   Well, in a way, the mono-issue logic of 'no alternative' is the problem we are skirting, but I don't want to let the masses off the hook by presuming they are always miserable. What about the erosion of Trade Union Power, and a distrust in Labour Unions generally? People aren't supporting them anymore because in recent years they became petty schoolyards. Workplaces are the new byword for 'stress' in many people's lives, where middle management, brand management and decadent lobbyists have more power as 'gatekeepers'.

KERRIGAN.   Well the problem, and I am sorry to say, is worse than that. The workers have been betrayed. You are talking about the corruption of power, but there's also just the corruption of money and status that affects everyone individually. So one of the things that happened is that when they started creating the Trade Unions, initially it was a volunteer organization. And then of course when they did begin to achieve success people said, 'We'll have people working full time on

---

53. See Chantal Mouffe, *For a Left Populism*, London: Verso 2018, p 47-48: 'the left populist strategy is not an avatar of the 'extreme left' but a different way of envisaging the rupture with neoliberalism through the recovery and radicalization of democracy. The current moves by the defenders of the status quo to label all of the critiques of the neoliberal order 'extreme left', and to present them as a danger to democracy, is a disingenuous attempt to impede any kind of challenge to the hegemonic order.'

EXT. BUSY STREET – DAYTIME

it.' Initially the idea was that there'd be people who would go for a year, or two years, or three years. But then they made it a career job. In fact, my father was a Trade Union Official in the 1950s and early 60s.

ROBINSON. Ah, that was his background before being a Labour parliamentarian and Lord Mayor?

KERRIGAN. That was his career. Then because of the logic of this Trade Union career they said, 'Well, we believe in good conditions for workers so as workers we employee ourselves as Trade Union Officials, and the representatives should have proper conditions.' So they did. So that managerial hierarchy, that bureaucracy developed with good conditions and a good pension, and some of them were politically and socially active. My father was very engaged. But the very nature of this career meant that Trade Union management was now cut off from the very workers they were representing.

ROBINSON. They were no longer workers.

KERRIGAN. They were no longer on the shop floor but they were driving around in nice cars in the 60s and 70s. Then came National Wage Agreements.

ROBINSON. What were they again?

KERRIGAN. Wage controls basically, when the government became the mediator and eliminated local negotiations. The union officials now lost a meaningful role, and led to them representing union membership as a form of individual job insurance. It was a kind of satirization of 'there is no alternative'. There is no unity; there is no such thing as society.

ROBINSON. Thatcherism and the throwing away of 'one for all and all for one'...

KERRIGAN. ...So the unions effectively destroyed themselves.

ROBINSON. So we've come full circle again, back to this idea of a need for a plural politics. Maybe what I saw then in *Gay's Against Imperialism: For Gay Liberation through National Liberation* was a populist impulse.

KERRIGAN. How populist?

ROBINSON. That it was *through* the liberation of the other. To be clear though, I feel that on *both* sides of the left and right divide, the word 'populism' shouldn't become the media's new byword for the racism and discrimination of the alt-right. Just call things what they are. Nigel Farage's campaigns are not populist: they are xenophobic, racist, hypocritical and imperialist. I mean populist in the sense of uniting a *polis*, the *demos* that in democracy decides. We were just talking a few moments ago about how in the last decades there seems to just have been a focus on celebrating those whose visibility and problems are dealt with because of their socio-economic success; but *Gays Against Imperialism* was a call for liberation *through* a broader liberation…

KERRIGAN. …*Against Imperialism*, yes.

ROBINSON. Why does imperialism keep coming back as the only word for something that we are constantly skirting but can never fully confront? The conflict between the social economy and the political elements of the movement in the Irish Queer Archive seemed fresh, and somehow familiar to me, reading it how many years later?

KERRIGAN. Nearly four decades. But the 1980s does feel close, the forever last decade.

ROBINSON. Watch out, things have gotten very 90s again, without the optimism, money or 'harmless' irony. This 'centre of nothing to decide but we will manipulate you into it anyway' needs to go. Now I am thinking back to your detailed memory about the sequencing, *Gays Against Imperialism*. It was one of the first things you told me on the phone.

EXT. BUSY STREET – DAYTIME

KERRIGAN. That the sequencing of the words was very important, and now, here we are, four years later...

ROBINSON. Gaze Against Imperialism!

CHART OF MAIN LGBTQ ORGANIZATIONS REFERRED TO
WITH (PROXIMITY) LINKAGES BY CATHAL KERRIGAN

	CGC Cork Gay Collective 1979-1988 | Lesbians & Gays	(Irish) Women's Liberation Movement 1970-1973 |
Sexual Freedoms Union 1973-1975 |	Against H-Block / Armagh 1980-1981 |	IWU Irish Women United 1975-1977 |
IGRM Irish Gay Rights Movement 1974-1983 |	GAI Gays Against Imperialism 1982-1984 |	LIL Liberation for Irish Lesbians 1978-1985 |
NIGRA Northern Ireland Gay Rights Association 1976-to date |	Belfast Lesbians & Gays Against Imperialism 1982-1985 |	Cork Lesbian Collective 1980-1987 |
NLGF National Lesbian & Gay Federation 1978-to date |	DLGC Dublin Lesbian & Gay Collectives 1982-1986 |	LOT Lesbians Organising Together 1991-to date |
GCN Gay Community News (magazine) 1987-to date |	GAA Gays Against the Amendment 1982-1983 |	LinC Lesbians in Cork 1995-to date |
Marriage Equality 2009-2013 |	GHA Gay Health Action 1985-1990 |	KAL Katherine & AnnLouise Advocacy 2004-2013 |

GLEN -- GAY & LESBIAN EQUALITY NETWORK -- 1988-2017

|
Yes Equality
2013-2015

Detail Index

Page 10

The Quare Fellow, written by Brendan Behan,
Stratford Theatre Production directed by
Joan Littlewood, 1956.

Courtesy Murray Melvin in memory
of Brendan Behan, Archives –
Theatre Royal Stratford East

Page 16, Page 18-19

Letters to the Editor
section published
in the The Irish Times,
31.08.81
01.09.81
06.10.81

ProQuest Historical
Newspapers

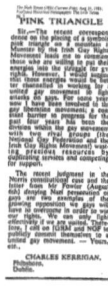

Page 26

Charles Self Murder Investigation
leaflet issued in February 1982
by the National Gay Federation.

Courtesy Irish Queer Archive,
National Library of Ireland

Page 29

Photocopied page from the Sunday World
newspaper, Ireland, published 20.03.83

Courtesy Irish Queer Archive, National
Library of Ireland

Detail Index

Page 31

Detail of Cork Gay Collective collage of photographs by Dónal Sheehan, 1983

Courtesy Kieran Rose

Page 35

Leaflet issued by Gays Against Amendment (GAA) in 1983 during the Anti-8th Amendment Campaign, calling on 'gays' to vote no in the upcoming referendum.

Courtesy Irish Queer Archive, National Library of Ireland

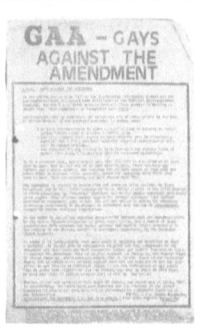

Page 39

Page 3 of Joni Crone's hand written and drawn pamphlet 'Gay Days and Nights of he Rountable: How to slay the minute-dragon and matters arising (or the structure of the NGF Administrative Council)', 1983.

Courtesy Irish Queer Archive, National Library of Ireland

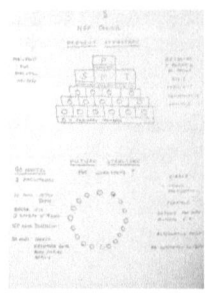

Page 49

Cathal Kerrigan speaking at Fairview March, 19.03.83.

Courtesy Cathal Kerrigan

Page 57

19.11.80. Document detailing gathering at Glencree Reconciliation Centre. The organisational body of this reconciliation initiative would go on to become the Cork Gay Collective.

Courtesy Kieran Rose

Page 60

Northern Ireland politicians John Hume and Bernadette McAliskey (née Devlin) on RTÉ's general election results coverage broadcast 12.06.81.

Courtesy RTÉ Archives

Page 63

23.01.82 demonstration march to the Belgian embassy protesting the teaching ban of Éliane Morissens, The Hague, Holland

Courtesy Anefo, Nationaal Archief, Netherlands

Page 72

Belfast Gays Against Imperialism, August 1984.

Courtesy Cathal Kerrigan

Detail Index   162.

Page 75, Page 76-77

Comité de soutien à Éliane
Morissens, Les Bulletins du
GRIF, n°6, 1982. Université
des femmes. Bulletin 6.
pp. 15-16. Translated
by Olivier Jorrot.

Creative Commons License

Page 86

Press Release, 13.05.81
by Charles Kerrigan, President
of Student Union 1981, University
of Cork.

National Library of Ireland,
Dublin

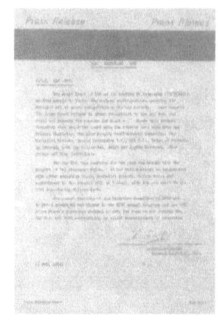

Page 101

Letter to Cathal (Charles) Kerrigan
from Taoiseach Charles Haughey
regarding raid at Windsor Avenue
Dublin and subsequent detention.

Courtesy Cathal Kerrigan

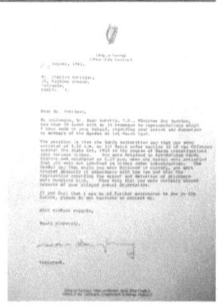

Page 103

Gays Against Imperialism
Launching Rally Poster,
02.04.82.

Courtesy Cathal Kerrigan

Page 109

Page 18 from the feminist pamphlet
'Images from the Armagh Picket', 1982.

Courtesy Irish Queer Archive, National
Library of Ireland

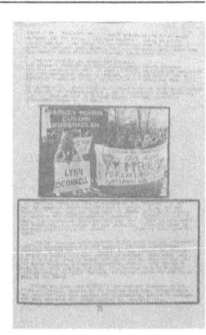

Page 113

Cathal Kerrigan, Politics of AIDS
Poster, Irish Critical Studies Group,
1986.

Courtesy Cathal Kerrigan

Pge 121

Mario Mieli (left), Lo scrittore
Mario Mieli e Guido Tosi a Milano
per la sceneggiatura di Una favola
spinta – 1982.

https://commons.wikimedia.org/wiki/
File:Mario_Mieli_e_Guido_Tosi.JPG

Page 123

Simon Nkoli interviewed by Chris
Vogel. Broadcast 03.10.89 on
Coming Out!, a cable television
program produced by the Winnipeg
Gay Media Collective, Canada.

Courtesy Manitoba Archives and
Special Collections, University
of Manitoba

Detail Index

Page 129

Film still, *Simon and I*, directed by Bev Ditsie and Nicky Newman.

Courtesy Women Make Movies
http://www.wmm.com/filmcatalog/press/siandi_presskit.pdf.
Permission granted by
Nicky Newman and Bev Ditsie.

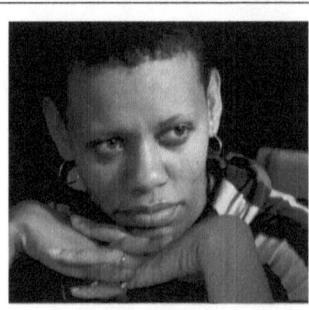

Page 142

Leaflet calling for protest against Justice Gannon's judgement around the murder of Declan Flynn, who, at the family's wishes, is not named in the 19.03.83 protest leaflet.

Colophon

Gaze Against Imperialism
by Padraig Robinson

© Metaflux Publishing 2019

ISBN: 978-0-9933272-7-8

Commissioning editor:
Rodrigo Maltez Novaes

Graphic Design:
Yin Yin Wong

A Quare Invisibility (PR) proofing:
Polly Gannon and Sarah Jones

Scenes with Cathal Kerrigan (PR/CK) edited in conversation with Cathal Kerrigan from audio transcripts recorded 2015–2018 in Cork, Berlin and Amsterdam

French to English translation:
Olivier Jorrot

Thank you to Ann, Arthur, the Arts Council Ireland, Asma, Beth, Breda, Bev, Cathal, Dijana, Dominique, Donal, Dylan, Elizabeth, Eric, Gouri, Isabella, Jaime, Jasmijn, Joan, Karen, KCC Arts Office, Kieran, Kris, Laois Arthouse, Laurie, Lisette, Mairtín, Martin, Mary, National Library of Ireland, Nicky, Nikolay, Olivier, Paul, Polly, Rachel, Rodrigo, Sarah, Sue, Xhercis, Yin Yin